SOUP & COMFORT

SOUP & COMFORT

A COOKBOOK OF HOMEMADE
RECIPES TO WARM THE SOUL

PAMELA ELLGEN

SONOMA
PRESS

Sonoma Press publishes its books in a variety of electronic and print formats. Some content that appears in print may not be available in electronic books, and vice versa.

Front cover photograph © StockFood/Condé Nast Collection; back cover photographs © StockFood/Malgorzata Stepien (Left), Stocksy/Darren Muir (middle), StockFood/Gräfe & Unzer Verlag/Grossmann.Schuerle (right); Interior photographs © Stocksy/Darren Muir, p. 2, 60, 67, 214; Stocksy/Miquel Llonch, p. 5; Stocksy/Alberto Bogo, p. 6; Stocksy/Vera Lair, p. 8; Stocksy/Aberto Bogo, p. 11; StockFood/Jalag/Wolfgang Schardt, p. 12; StockFood/Clive Streeter, p. 24, 110; Stocksy/Lee Avison, p. 26; StockFood /Great Stock!, p. 33; StockFood/Helen Cathcart, p. 40; StockFood/Bernhard Winkelmann, p. 47; StockFood/Gräfe & Unzer Verlag/Grossmann.Schuerle, p. 52; StockFood/Linda Pugliese, p. 74; StockFood/Boch Photography, p. 88; Stocksy/Melanie Defazio, p. 93; Gareth Morgans/StockFood, p. 98; StockFood/Malgorzata Stepien, p. 123; StockFood/Tanya Zouev, p. 134; Stocksy/Jeff Wasserman, p. 138; StockFood/Studio Lipov, p. 145; StockFood/Gräfe & Unzer Verlag/Coco Lang, p. 154; StockFood/Gareth Morgans, p. 166, 184; StockFood/Ian Garlick, p. 177; StockFood/Renée Comet, p. 194; Stocksy/Andrijana Kostova, p. 203; Stocksy/Sara Remington, p. 224; Author photo © 2015 by Rich Ellgen

TRADEMARKS: Sonoma Press and the Sonoma Press logo are trademarks or registered trademarks of Arcas Publishing, a Callisto Media Inc. company and/or its affiliates, in the United States and other countries, and may not be used without written permission. All other trademarks are the property of their respective owners. Sonoma Press is not associated with any product or vendor mentioned in this book.

ISBN: Print 978-1-943451-00-5
eBook 978-1-943451-01-2

SOUPS THAT NOURISH
EVERYBODY'S SOULS

The soups in this book provide comfort on so many levels, not only in the traditional emotional sense—the "sweater weather, cozy fire, and a steaming bowl of chicken soup" sort of way—but also in that they're brimming with healthy, affordable ingredients that everyone can enjoy.

Classics—Creamy Tomato Soup (page 63) and Rainy Day Chicken Noodle Soup (page 95) are just what the doctor ordered.

Vegetarian and Vegan—Fire-Roasted Vegan Chili (page 179) and French Onion Soup (page 182) made with Roasted Vegetable Broth (page 29) are tantalizing, meat-free options.

Food Allergy Friendly—New England Clam Chowder (page 122) can be yours in a dairy- and gluten-free version.

Paleo—Cuban-Style Chicken Stew (page 162) and Oktoberfest Stew with Apples, Sausage & Sweet Potatoes (page 146) give you something to sink your teeth into.

Low-Sodium or Low-Calorie—Roasted Butternut Squash Soup with Sage (page 68) and the lightened-up Cheesy Chicken Enchilada Soup (page 152) are two new companions that you'll adore.

The Rest of the Best—Basic Beef Stew (page 140) straight out of the slow cooker is a perfect way to enjoy your evening.

CONTENTS

INTRODUCTION

IN the children's book *Mouse Soup*, a shrewd mouse outwits a weasel who is about to make soup out of him. "You must fill the soup with stories!" the mouse says. "Or, it will not taste good."

Soup tastes better with stories. So, in this book I've shared my stories of cooking and family and those times when the recipe didn't go as planned. Once, when my husband, Rich, and I had just started dating, he rode his motorcycle over 100 miles in the rain and came back soaked through and freezing. I made him a big pot of vegetarian chili but discovered midway through cooking that I didn't have any bell peppers and used canned jalapeño peppers measure for measure instead. "Hot" doesn't even begin to describe this chili. It took him and his roommate several days to make it through the whole pot, drowning it in sour cream, shredded cheese, and corn bread with copious amounts of water to chase it down. We survived that little adventure, and you, too, will recover from any cooking "surprises" that might come your way.

I recently rediscovered the comforting power of soup while trying to find just one dish that could feed my whole family. In my house, each person has a different dietary restriction. Rich doesn't eat meat, my kids cannot eat dairy or wheat, and I opt for a Paleo-style diet. With all of these parameters, I had resorted to cooking separate meals on many nights. Some evenings I fed the kids first and then sent them to bed. Afterward, I set about cooking a second meal for my husband and me. We often didn't eat until 9 p.m.! Our grocery budget was burgeoning, our sink was piled with dishes, and I missed sharing meals together as a family. Clearly, it wasn't working.

Fortunately, when I began researching and testing recipes for this book, I realized that soup was the answer to our dinnertime dilemma. It was the simple solution that had been there all along. I began with the Brazilian Fish Stew (page 133) and then created Curried Sweet Potato Soup (page 62). My oldest son tasted it and said, "Oh, yum! People are going to love this!" In that moment, I knew I had found the one meal that would satisfy everyone—both my family and yours! One pot. One dinner. One happy family.

Soup dinners also allowed me to do some of the preparation in advance, freeing me up to spend more quality time with my family and less time in the kitchen.

When soup is made from scratch, you can add or omit whatever suits your family's needs. Gone are the days of turning over a can and putting it back on the shelf because it's full of things you cannot eat (not to mention a generous dose of preservatives). There's something so comforting about knowing exactly what's going into your meal . . . and what isn't.

I created each of these soup recipes to cater to a wide variety of dietary restrictions and taste preferences, from vegan and vegetarian to Paleo and allergen-free. No one should be left out! Each recipe utilizes easily accessible, fresh, whole-food ingredients, too. No bouillon cubes here! I've also kept cost in mind. Soup is a great way to stretch your grocery budget, so most recipes use affordable ingredients you likely already have in your kitchen. In addition, I offer handy substitutions. If you need to refresh your memory about any of the terms used in this book, go straight to the Glossary (page 228) to find straightforward explanations.

Whether you're a family of one or serving a tribe, soups are inherently easy to divide or multiply so you can make just the right amount. They also make excellent leftovers, and extras can be a comforting gift to bring a new neighbor or a sick friend.

Soups are easily adaptable to each season, whether chilled on a hot summer afternoon or piping hot on a cold wintry evening. My summertime favorites include Corn Chowder with Pickled Jalapeños (page 174) and Gazpacho (page 42). In the fall and winter, I like to curl up with a bowl of Cioppino Seafood Stew (page 114) or Oktoberfest Stew with Apples, Sausage & Sweet Potatoes (page 146).

In writing this book, I have found that homemade soup is nourishment for both the body and soul—comfort food at its finest! May you have heartwarming experiences of your own as you try out the recipes on these pages. Remember to fill the soups with stories of your own. Soup tastes better with stories. Find out for yourself.

1

SATISFYING SOUPS
FOR EVERYONE

On the first day of third grade for my oldest son, a cool marine layer of clouds blanketed our small California town. With steaming mugs of coffee in our hands, Rich and I walked to school with our son, ready to meet new teachers and see old friends, and I considered how much I love fall. It's a season of new beginnings and comforting nostalgia—somewhat like good, homemade soup. The best soup recipes are adapted to our changing tastes, the changing seasons, and our changing dietary needs, yet still grounded in generations of tradition. When I make soup from scratch, I'm filled with comfort knowing that I'm nourishing my family with every spoonful.

COMFORT IN A BOWL

For cooking newbies, soup is a comforting place to start. Many recipes in this book allow you to simply place all of the ingredients into one pot, turn on the heat, sit back, and wait for a delicious meal. So long as there is water in the pot, the risk of scorching food is virtually eliminated. Moreover, you can adjust the seasonings as you go, adding only a pinch of salt at a time until it's just right.

Soup takes the stress out of cooking for a busy family because you can make it ahead of time, allow it to cool in the refrigerator, and then reheat it when you're ready to serve. I love knowing dinner is already taken care of, allowing me to relax during the afternoon and hear about my family's day. After leaving my son with his teachers and classmates that first day of school, I came home and made the Roasted Garlic & 10-Bean Soup with Balsamic Reduction (page 170). As it simmered away, I even had time to roll out some gluten-free Paleo Sage Breadsticks (page 198) and let my youngest son help without fear of grease splattering or any need to rush food onto the table.

Of course, even better than getting tonight's dinner taken care of is the relief of knowing that you've also prepared tomorrow's lunch. Soup makes excellent leftovers, travels easily, and is easy to reheat. Store toppings in a separate container and you have a gourmet lunch right at your desk. Imagine how warm and happy your loved ones will feel when they enjoy a hot cup of your soup on their lunch break at work!

Did your mother ever tell you to chew your food more thoroughly? Mine, too! Fortunately, soups, especially the puréed varieties, are already broken down into easily digestible mouthfuls—a comfort to your belly. Soups are also hydrating, a boon both in hot summer months and during cold, dry winters.

Soup makes an excellent dinner to bring to a friend or new neighbor. Not only is it a comforting reminder that you care, but it also makes it easy for you to prepare dinner for your own family at the same time. Some friends even start soup clubs, allowing each person (in a four-member club) to prepare a meal once a month and deliver it to the others. Four dinners with just one night of cooking—I'm already planning my own soup club!

FROM STONE SOUP ᴛᴏ SOUP KITCHENS: SOUP AND SERVICE

In *Stone Soup*, the classic fable, hungry travelers convince villagers to share their food by placing a stone in a kettle and asking for just a little garnish. One by one each of the villagers contributes whatever he or she has: a few carrots, a leek, or a hunk of bread. By pooling their resources, they create a delicious meal. Although the story varies widely throughout global cultures, one theme emerges—soup can be made with whatever you have on hand and easily expands to feed a lot of people.

Count Rumford is credited with creating the first soup kitchen in the 1800s to feed Bavarian military personnel. Later, he was tasked with creating a nutritionally dense and inexpensive ration for feeding the poor. His basic recipe included pearl barley, dried peas, potatoes, water, salt, and vinegar or sour beer. In the 1930s, during the Great Depression in the United States, unemployment rates soared over 24 percent and soup kitchens became essential sources of nourishment.

Today, soup kitchens serve more than just soup, offering bread and meat and even food baskets for people enduring poverty or homelessness. Many philanthropic individuals volunteer in soup kitchens, especially around the holidays. However, most soup kitchens are open year-round and are eager for compassionate volunteers in all seasons.

For the past 20 years, my mother-in-law, Debbie, has opened her home to American servicemen and women stationed overseas. She offers much more than soup—her house is a home away from home for many young people who are away from their families for the first time. She shared a few of her recipes with me, some of which she's been cooking for decades. Try her Mexican Bean & Chicken Soup (page 149) and Cheesy Chicken Enchilada Soup (page 152) and share them with people who are new to your town.

Working in a soup kitchen may not be feasible for you, but why not share soup with the people in your community? You could take a meal to a new mom, invite new neighbors into your home for dinner, or merely prepare a comforting soup dinner for your family. Sharing soup can be a great way to warm the soul!

ESSENTIAL EQUIPMENT

Historically, the first soups were made by dropping hot stones into waterproof containers such as animal skins and clay pots. Today we have far more utensils, pots, pans, and appliances at our disposal. However, you need just a few handy tools to craft a delicious meal.

Indispensable Tools

4-quart stainless steel cooking pot. I have had the same cooking pot since I got married more than a decade ago. Its heavy bottom prevents foods from scorching, and it retains and transfers heat well. It holds enough soup to feed my own family of four and provide one or two portions of leftovers.

Immersion blender. An immersion blender allows you to purée your soup without removing it from the pot. Transferring hot soup to a traditional countertop blender is a dicey proposition. The blender pitcher holds too little liquid and the lid is not designed to contain hot liquids, which may result in splatters and burns.

Metal soup ladle. A metal soup ladle allows you to serve a good ratio of broth to vegetables and meat. Using a regular metal spoon doesn't allow you to get enough broth. Alternatively, pouring soup directly from the pot usually results in splashing and too much broth in the first few bowls.

Wire whisk. When making a roux (with flour and butter), a wire whisk helps break up any lumps. It also evenly distributes the roux into the broth or milk added later.

Wooden spoon. I prefer cooking with wooden spoons because, unlike metal spoons, they do not retain heat, and, unlike plastic spoons, they do not disperse chemicals into the food.

Helpful Equipment

China cap. This cone-shaped, metal strainer is particularly good for making puréed soups.

8-quart stainless steel cooking pot. When you want to double one of the soup recipes in this book, use an 8-quart cooking pot.

Glass mason jars for storing leftovers. They travel easily and are heat-proof, allowing you to microwave them if you wish (make sure to remove the lid) or pour the soup into a small saucepan for reheating. They're a better option than plastic, especially for hot foods that may leach chemicals from the plastic.

Slow cooker. Some soups are especially well suited for a slow cooker, allowing you to do all of the prep work ahead of time and have a delicious dinner ready and waiting several hours later. They can also be left unattended, making them particularly appealing to working professionals.

 FIX-AND-FORGET SOUPS

Most of the recipes in this book are made in a traditional stockpot, but many can be made in a 4-quart slow cooker. These recipes feature a "fix-and-forget" label and offer a tip explaining how to use a slow cooker to prepare the soup.

SOUP LOVER'S PANTRY

One of my favorite things about cooking from scratch is that I get to choose each and every ingredient that goes into my food and in what quantities. It's so empowering to decide how much salt to use, to swap allergens for safe ingredients in classic recipes, and to fill soup with fresh, high-quality ingredients. Keep the following staples in your pantry (and refrigerator) in order to easily create the recipes in this book.

Butter is used to make roux and to impart warm, rich flavors, especially for finishing puréed soups.

Canned whole plum tomatoes are available year-round and have more flavor than diced canned tomatoes.

Carrots have a long shelf life in the refrigerator and lend texture and sweetness to many soup recipes.

Celery has a long shelf life in the refrigerator and imparts texture, complexity, and umami.

Coconut milk is used in many Asian-style soups and as a dairy-free alternative to heavy cream. If you can find it, coconut cream is an even more suitable replacement for heavy cream.

 MIREPOIX

Mirepoix (meer-pwah) is composed of two parts diced onions, one part diced celery, and one part diced carrots. It is used in French cooking as the basis for a wide variety of dishes, including soups.

Dried legumes, such as black beans, kidney beans, chickpeas, and lentils, are called for in many recipes. I prefer to use dried beans because soaking them before cooking improves their digestibility.

Leeks have a more subtle flavor and texture than onions and are used in many soup recipes in this book.

Olive oil is used to cook meat and vegetables and as a finishing oil for many soups.

Onions are an essential vegetable in many soups and have a relatively long shelf life. However, do not store them near potatoes, which will accelerate spoilage.

Potatoes are puréed into some soups to thicken them and are diced and cooked into others. They have a long shelf life when stored in a cool, dark place.

Red wine is used in some recipes for flavor and complexity. I use an inexpensive cabernet, zinfandel, or pinot noir depending on the recipe.

Rice is used in some grain-based recipes and as a side or filler in other recipes. I typically use white rice because it is easily digestible and I prefer the texture. Wild rice is another pleasing alternative.

Sea salt is the only salt I use in my kitchen, both white and the pink Himalayan variety. It is minimally processed and contains trace minerals and elements without any additives to prevent clumping. Kosher salt is an acceptable substitute when sea salt is called for.

Vinegar is added to stocks to help bones release nutrients and to soups at the end of cooking to balance the flavors. If you don't have the vinegar called for in a particular recipe, feel free to substitute the closest equivalent in color.

ROUX

To make a roux, combine equal parts butter and flour in a saucepan over medium heat and whisk until thick and bubbling. The roux can be added to soups to thicken them, or liquid can be added directly to the roux all at once. Whisk constantly to break up any lumps and cook for at least four minutes to remove the starchy taste of the flour. To make a gluten- and dairy-free roux, cook equal parts palm shortening and sorghum flour over medium-low heat using the same method. Both versions of roux work well for thickening soups, gumbo, chicken potpie, and soufflé.

SOUP, SODIUM, AND SEASONING

Cooking soup from scratch is particularly important if you're watching your sodium intake. Canned soups are often loaded with salt to make up for inferior ingredients. Low-sodium varieties are hardly better—there's less salt, so you just have to suffer through the bland concoction. Early in your "soup from scratch" adventure, you will discover how delicious homemade soup can be, even without loads of salt.

Here are a few tips for getting the most flavor with the least amount of sodium:

- Use homemade broths and stocks, which have an immense amount of flavor and only as much salt as you've already added to them.
- Wait until the soup has neared the end of cooking to add salt. The soup will reduce as it cooks, allowing the flavors to intensify. It may not need as much salt as you think.
- Use fresh herbs, lemon juice, freshly ground black pepper, a small pinch of sugar, vinegar, and other flavorful ingredients to season the soup without salt.

INGREDIENT SWAPS FOR DIETARY RESTRICTIONS

The goal of this book is to make soup accessible for everyone, regardless of dietary restrictions. I encourage you to get comfortable with making food-related adjustments for the benefit of your health. Here are several common ingredients that you may wish to swap with diet-friendly substitutions.

Bacon or bacon grease is often used as a flavor base for soups. I have used liquid smoke to achieve a similar flavor. It works especially well in clam chowder. Smoked paprika also works well in tomato-based soups.

Beef can be replaced with chunks of portobello mushrooms: simply reduce cooking time. Replace beef broth with Roasted Vegetable Broth (page 29).

Butter may be problematic for many people, including vegans and those with dairy allergies. When used in a roux, it can be replaced with canola oil or palm shortening. When used for seasoning, it can be replaced with a pinch of sea salt. Some people find that ghee butter is easier to tolerate than regular butter because it contains virtually no lactose and casein. Ghee is the closest substitute, flavor-wise, since it is made from butter.

Chicken can be replaced with seitan, which has a similar texture, or tofu. Beans or vegetables are another alternative. Replace chicken broth with Roasted Vegetable Broth (page 29).

Heavy cream contains milk fat and some lactose and casein, which may be problematic for people with dairy allergies. Coconut milk or coconut cream are suitable replacements.

Noodles typically contain wheat and are not Paleo. They can be replaced with zucchini noodles or simply omitted.

Rice and grains can be simply omitted from some recipes or replaced with riced cauliflower.

Soy sauce is not Paleo and soy is a common allergen. It can be replaced with gluten-free fish sauce, coconut aminos, and even a pinch of sea salt.

Substitution Summary

FOOD	SUBSTITUTION
Bacon	Liquid smoke, smoked paprika
Beef	Mushrooms
Butter	Canola oil, palm shortening, sea salt, ghee
Chicken	Seitan, tofu, vegetables, beans
Heavy cream	Coconut milk, coconut cream
Noodles	Zucchini noodles
Rice	Riced cauliflower
Soy sauce	Gluten-free fish sauce, coconut aminos, sea salt
Wheat flour	Gluten-free flour, white rice flour, potato starch, sorghum flour
White wine	Water with lemon juice or apple cider vinegar

Wheat flour is problematic for people with wheat allergies and those who are unable to tolerate gluten. Many gluten-free flours exist, but not all achieve the same function as flour in soups. Potato starch, sorghum flour, and white rice flour work well as thickeners. Simply dissolve them in about ¼ cup of broth or water and add this slurry to the soup to prevent clumps.

White wine can be omitted from recipes and replaced with water and a squeeze of lemon juice or apple cider vinegar. It can also be replaced with broth or stock.

EASY PEASY SOUPS

Here are a few tips and tricks I employ to save time, money, and effort when making soups.

Chop vegetables ahead of time. Or you can purchase pre-chopped vegetables from the grocery store to save time during the dinner hour.

Make a double batch of broth. Freeze the second batch for later use.

Mix spices. For curries and chilies that require several spices, mix the spices together ahead of time and store them in a jar. I like to make several times the quantity that I'll need for one batch of soup so the spices are ready and waiting the next time I need them.

Soak beans overnight. Rinse and drain the beans in the morning, and then cook them on the back burner while you make breakfast. Store in the refrigerator until ready to use.

Use vegetable and meat scraps. These make flavorful stocks and broths. Simply save them in the freezer until you have enough.

SOUP ON THE GO

Bone broth is the new green smoothie because it makes a convenient, portable breakfast. Simply heat it and pour into a stainless steel thermos to enjoy during your commute or at your desk. For homemade bone broth, follow the recipes for Roasted Chicken Stock (see page 31) or Beef Stock (see page 35) using a large slow cooker instead of the stove. Cook the broth on low for 24 to 48 hours, skimming the foam every few hours and adding water as needed to keep the ingredients covered. The broth will be ready when it's dark and flavorful.

SEASONAL SOUPS

This cookbook offers soups that are particularly well-suited for taking advantage of seasonal ingredients. Here are some of my favorites for each season:

Summer

Corn Chowder with
Pickled Jalapeños
page 174

Pork Chili Verde
page 159

Cucumber Melon Soup
page 54

Winter

Venison Stew
page 148

Broccoli Cheese Soup
page 183

Beef Stout Stew with
Herbed Dumplings
page 156

Fall

Roasted Butternut Squash
Soup with Sage
page 68

Oktoberfest Stew with Apples,
Sausage & Sweet Potatoes
page 146

Butternut Squash & Cauliflower
Curry with Coconut Yogurt
page 168

Spring

Kale, Cannellini Bean
& Sausage Soup
page 142

Cream of Watercress Soup
page 75

Mint & Pea Soup
page 49

SEASONAL SOUPS, TIMELESS SOUPS

Soups can and should be enjoyed year-round, not just in winter. I love making both sweet and savory chilled soups in the summer, but hot and spicy soups are equally delicious. In the fall, I crave the flavors of the season, especially apple, pumpkin, and butternut squash. Winter is a good time to use up root vegetables and enjoy meaty curries. The springtime offers another opportunity to make use of seasonal ingredients, such as delicate greens and peas.

SECRETS FOR SALVAGING SOUPS

Uh-oh, you just tasted your favorite chicken soup and it's a bit too salty. Don't worry! It's not a complete loss. Here are a few remedies for common soup ailments:

Too Salty Unfortunately, sticking a piece of bread or potatoes into the soup won't fix the problem. But you can balance the salty flavor with a splash of vinegar or lemon juice (except for dairy-based soups) or a pinch of sugar. Alternately, toss in a starch like rice or noodles to soak up excess salt, and then pour in additional broth, wine, water, or milk, depending on the type of soup.

Too Thick If your soup is too thick, you can easily thin it with additional broth or milk, depending on the type of soup. Avoid adding acidic liquid, such as lemon juice or wine, to a dairy-based soup.

Too Thin If your soup is too thin, make a wet paste of wheat flour, potato starch, or white rice flour dissolved in a few tablespoons of water. Whisk it into the soup and bring to a gentle simmer until it thickens.

Bland Your taste buds can sense at least five different flavors: salty, sour, sweet, bitter, and umami. Umami is present in monosodium glutamate (MSG), as well as many natural ingredients such as mushrooms and celery. If your soup is bland, it's likely that at least one of these flavors is missing. Taste your soup and consider which of the key flavors might be missing, then add either ¼ teaspoon of red chili flakes, a splash of vinegar, a pinch of sugar, or a dash of salt.

STORAGE *and* THAWING TIPS

All of the soups in this book include information on how long they can be stored.

To store leftovers, chill your soup thoroughly in the refrigerator uncovered. You can accelerate the cooling process by stirring it occasionally. Once it is thoroughly chilled, cover the container and store it for as long as indicated in the recipe.

To store soup in the freezer, pour it into zip-top plastic freezer bags and freeze the bags on their sides. Stand the bags upright once the soup is completely frozen. To thaw frozen soups quickly, place them in a bath of cool water for 30 minutes, then pour or scoop them into a pot and warm them over medium-low heat.

Chilled soups made with fresh greens and dairy-based soups don't freeze very well. The same goes for fish stews, unless you separate the fish from the broth and store it in a separate bag. Bring the liquid portion of the soup to a simmer first and then add the fish during the last few minutes of reheating.

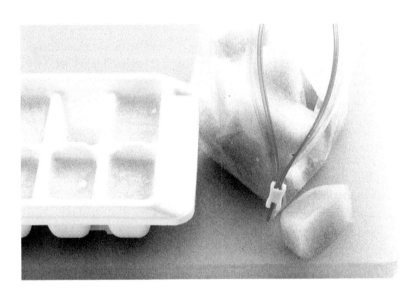

Recipe Labels

LABEL	EXPLANATION
Paleo	Free from grain, dairy, legumes, white potatoes, and refined sugar.
Paleo-Friendly	Substitution tip provided to make the recipe free from grain, dairy, legumes, white potatoes, industrial oils, and refined sugar.
Vegetarian	Free from meat, poultry, and fish.
Vegan	Free from meat, poultry, fish, and animal-derived ingredients including dairy, eggs, and honey.
Gluten-Free	Free from wheat, barley, rye, triticale, and ingredients derived from these grains.
Big 8 Allergen–Friendly	Free from milk, eggs, fish, shellfish, tree nuts, peanuts, wheat, and soy.
Fix-and-Forget	You can easily make the soup in a slow cooker; the instructions will give you a time estimate.

Nutritional Information For recipes in which a range of servings is given, nutritional information is calculated according to the largest serving size. When the recipe says it yields four to six servings, the nutritional information is based on four servings.

2
STOCKS, BROTHS
& CLEAR SOUPS

BASIC VEGETABLE BROTH

YIELD VARIES **PREP** 5 MINS **COOK** 2 HOURS

■ PALEO ■ GLUTEN-FREE ■ VEGAN ■ BIG 8 ALLERGEN—FRIENDLY ■ FIX-AND-FORGET

This scrappy little vegetable broth is the frugal cook's secret weapon. It costs pennies to make and uses food that otherwise would have been thrown away. I save vegetable ends and herb stems in a container in the freezer over several days or weeks and make the broth just before I need it. These vegetables are the ones I tend to have around, but use whatever you have and aim for about 2 cups of vegetables per 1 quart of water.

Onion pieces
Carrot pieces
Celery ends and leaves
Leek ends and greens
Bell pepper cores
Tomato cores
Mushroom stems
Garlic pieces
Thyme sprigs
Parsley stems
Sea salt
Red wine vinegar

1 In a large pot, mix together the onion, carrot, celery, leek, bell pepper, tomato, mushroom, garlic, thyme, and parsley. Season with salt and fill the pot with cold water. Cover the pot with a lid and bring to a simmer over medium-low heat. Cook for 1 hour, then remove the lid and allow the broth to reduce for another hour.

2 Using a metal strainer, pour the mixture into a heat-proof container, pressing on the vegetables to release stored moisture. Season with salt and a splash of red wine vinegar.

3 Use immediately or chill completely and then store in a covered container in the refrigerator for up to 3 days or in the freezer for 3 months.

VARIATION TIP: You can use almost any vegetables or herbs you have in your kitchen, though brassicas, winter squashes, and fennel tend to be overpowering. Also, skip ginger and chiles, unless you're going for a spicy broth.

FIX-AND-FORGET: To make this soup in a slow cooker, simply place all of the ingredients in a 4-quart slow cooker and cook on low for 6 hours or on high for 2 hours.

ROASTED VEGETABLE BROTH

YIELD 2 QUARTS   **PREP** 10 MINS   **COOK** 1 HOUR, 35 MINS

■ PALEO ■ GLUTEN-FREE ■ VEGAN ■ BIG 8 ALLERGEN–FRIENDLY

For many years, I avoided recipes that called for chicken broth, because I found no suitable store-bought vegetarian replacement. But at last, chicken broth has met its match! Roasting vegetables before you make this vegetable broth intensifies their sweetness and imparts a complex umami flavor to the broth.

2 onions, sliced into thick rings
2 carrots, cut into 2-inch pieces
2 celery stalks, cut into 2-inch pieces
1 cup halved mushrooms
4 garlic cloves, peeled
2 tablespoons olive oil
1 thyme sprig
1 rosemary sprig
Sea salt
½ cup dry white wine
3 quarts water

1 Preheat the oven to 375°F.

2 Line a sheet pan with parchment paper and then spread the onions, carrots, celery, mushrooms, and garlic out on it. Drizzle with olive oil. Roast uncovered for 35 minutes, or until the vegetables are beginning to brown.

3 In a large pot, mix together the roasted vegetables, thyme, rosemary, a generous pinch of sea salt, wine, and water. Bring to a simmer over medium heat and allow the liquid to reduce for about 1 hour.

4 Using a metal strainer, pour the mixture into a heat-proof container.

5 Store in a covered container in the refrigerator for up to 3 days or in the freezer for 3 months.

SUBSTITUTION TIP: If you prefer not to use wine in this broth, simply omit it and stir in 1 teaspoon of apple cider vinegar or red wine vinegar after the broth has been strained.

Nutritional Information (1 cup) Calories: 46; Saturated Fat: 1g; Carbohydrates: 1g; Sodium: 34mg; Fiber: 0g; Protein: 0g

PARMESAN BROTH

YIELD 2 QUARTS **PREP** 5 MINS **COOK** 1 HOUR

■ GLUTEN-FREE ■ VEGETARIAN ■ FIX-AND-FORGET

This hearty vegetarian broth is perfect for risotto and vegetarian bean soups, or anywhere you might otherwise use chicken broth. It's especially delicious in Saffron, Garlic & Potato Soup (page 186). Like the Basic Vegetable Broth, this recipe makes use of food scraps that might otherwise go to waste. Simply save your Parmesan rinds in the freezer along with the green portions of leeks and mushroom stems until you're ready to make the broth.

1½ cups Parmesan rinds
1 leek, green and pale green parts only
½ cup mushroom stems
1 thyme sprig
1 garlic clove, peeled
3 quarts water
Sea salt

FIX-AND-FORGET: To make this soup in a slow cooker, simply place all of the ingredients in a 4-quart slow cooker and cook on low for 6 hours or on high for 2 hours.

1 In a large pot, mix together the Parmesan rinds, leek, mushroom stems, thyme, garlic, and water, and season with salt. Cover and cook for 30 minutes over medium-low heat. Remove the lid and continue cooking for another 30 minutes to reduce the liquid.

2 Using a metal strainer, pour the mixture into a heat-proof container, pressing on the vegetables and cheese rinds to release stored moisture.

3 Use immediately or chill completely and then store in a covered container in the refrigerator for up to 3 days or in the freezer for 3 months.

SUBSTITUTION TIP: Other hard cheeses will make a beautifully complex broth as well. Pecorino Romano and even hard Cheddar will work. Use what you have and pair the broth with the wide variety of soups and stews in this book.

Nutritional Information (1 cup) Calories: 25; Saturated Fat: 1g; Carbohydrates: 1g; Sodium: 65mg; Fiber: 0g; Protein: 1g

ROASTED CHICKEN STOCK

YIELD 2 QUARTS **PREP** 10 MINS **COOK** 2 HOURS, 30 MINS

▪ PALEO ▪ GLUTEN-FREE ▪ BIG 8 ALLERGEN–FRIENDLY

Roasting the chicken bones before you simmer them in water adds complexity and depth of flavor to this stock. I like to save the backbones of whole chickens in the freezer until I have enough to make this stock. Simply defrost in the refrigerator before roasting.

3 pounds chicken bones
1 onion, sliced into thick rings
2 carrots, halved
2 celery stalks, halved
2 bay leaves
3 quarts water

1 Preheat the oven to 450°F.

2 On a sheet pan, spread out the chicken bones. Roast uncovered for 30 minutes, or until thoroughly browned.

3 In a large pot, mix together the chicken bones, onion, carrots, celery, bay leaves, and water. Bring to a simmer over medium-low heat and cook for 2 hours, skimming off and discarding the foam from the surface.

4 Using a metal strainer, pour the mixture into a heat-proof container, pressing on the vegetables and chicken bones to release moisture.

5 Use immediately or chill completely and then store in a covered container in the refrigerator for up to 3 days or in the freezer for 3 months.

COOKING TIP: If you don't have chicken bones and prefer not to purchase a whole chicken, simply ask your butcher to save some bones for you. Per pound, the bones will cost a fraction of the price of a whole chicken.

Nutritional Information (1 cup) Calories: 86; Saturated Fat: 1g; Carbohydrates: 3g; Sodium: 54mg; Fiber: 0g; Protein: 3g

CHICKEN BROTH

YIELD 2 QUARTS **PREP** 10 MINS **COOK** 2 HOURS

■ PALEO ■ GLUTEN-FREE ■ BIG 8 ALLERGEN–FRIENDLY ■ FIX-AND-FORGET

The difference between *broth* and *stock* is the ratio of bones to meat used. Typically, broth is made with meat, bones, and other aromatic vegetables and herbs, whereas stock is made from clean bones. Stocks contain more gelatin and minerals than broth and thus have a fuller mouth feel that adds body to soups, stews, and pan sauces. This chicken broth offers the best of both worlds, beginning with a whole chicken and then removing the meat and allowing the broth to cook down with the bones.

1 whole 2- to 3-pound chicken
1 onion, sliced into thick rings
2 carrots, halved
2 celery stalks, halved
1 thyme sprig
6 garlic cloves, smashed
1 teaspoon peppercorns
1 bay leaf
½ teaspoon sea salt
½ teaspoon red wine vinegar
3 quarts water

1 In a large pot, mix together the chicken, onion, carrots, celery, thyme, garlic, peppercorns, bay leaf, sea salt, vinegar, and water. Cover the pot and bring the liquid to a simmer over medium heat.

2 Reduce the heat to keep the broth at a gentle simmer. Skim the foam from the surface of the broth and discard.

3 When the chicken is cooked through—this will take about 1 hour—remove it and place it on a cutting board. When it is cool enough to handle, remove the meat from the bones and reserve the meat for another use. Return the bones to the broth and continue cooking uncovered for another hour.

continued

4 Using a metal strainer, pour the mixture into a heat-proof container, pressing on the vegetables and chicken bones to release moisture.

5 Use immediately or chill completely and then store in a covered container in the refrigerator for up to 3 days or in the freezer for 3 months.

COOKING TIP: If you don't want to cook a whole chicken, simply use chicken bones, such as necks and backbones. Proceed with the recipe as written, leaving the bones in the pot for the entire cooking time and removing the lid from the pot halfway through.

Nutritional Information (1 cup) Calories: 104; Saturated Fat: 3g; Carbohydrates: 4g; Sodium: 104mg; Fiber: 0g; Protein: 7g

FIX-AND-FORGET: To make this soup in a slow cooker, simply place all of the ingredients in a 4-quart slow cooker and cook on low for 6 hours or on high for 2 hours.

BEEF STOCK

YIELD 2 QUARTS **PREP** 10 MINS **COOK** 3 HOURS, 15 MINS

■ PALEO ■ GLUTEN-FREE ■ BIG 8 ALLERGEN–FRIENDLY

Once you've tried homemade beef stock, you'll never go back to store-bought varieties again. I like to make a double batch and freeze half for later use in sauces, soups, and stews. This recipe serves as an excellent base for demi-glace or beef bourguignon.

3 pounds beef bones, cut into pieces
1 onion, sliced into thick rings
2 carrots, halved
2 celery stalks, halved
1 garlic head, halved horizontally
2 tablespoons olive oil
1 thyme sprig
1 rosemary sprig
2 bay leaves
2 cups dry red wine
3 quarts water
Sea salt

1 Preheat the oven to 450°F.

2 On a sheet pan, spread out the beef bones. Roast uncovered for 45 minutes, or until evenly browned. Add the onion, carrots, celery, garlic, and olive oil to the pan and continue roasting for another 30 minutes.

3 In a large pot, mix the roasted bones and vegetables with the thyme, rosemary, bay leaves, wine, and water. Season with salt. Bring to a simmer over medium-low heat and cook for 2 hours, skimming off and discarding the foam from the surface of the broth.

4 Using a metal strainer, pour the mixture into a heat-proof container, pressing on the vegetables and beef bones.

5 Use immediately or chill completely and then store in a covered container in the refrigerator for up to 3 days or in the freezer for 3 months.

COOKING TIP: It is very important to roast the beef bones before making this stock. Otherwise, it will have an acrid taste.

Nutritional Information (1 cup) Calories: 94; Saturated Fat: 1g; Carbohydrates: 3g; Sodium: 154mg; Fiber: 0g; Protein: 1g

STOCKS, BROTHS & CLEAR SOUPS

SEAFOOD STOCK

YIELD 2 QUARTS **PREP** 10 MINS **COOK** 30 MINS

■ PALEO ■ GLUTEN-FREE

Many seafood soup recipes, such as Cioppino Seafood Stew (page 114) and clam chowder (pages 122 and 125), call for chicken broth. But a homemade fish or seafood stock breathes an oceany depth into seafood soups and stews. You can also use it to poach fish or make the classic French velouté sauce. This recipe is based on Julia Child's Fumet de Poisson au Vin Blanc.

3 pounds fresh fish bones, trimmings, and heads
1 onion, sliced into thin rings
1 celery stalk, sliced into 2-inch pieces
1 cup dry white wine
Handful parsley stems
Squeeze of fresh lemon juice
2 quarts cold water
¼ teaspoon sea salt

1 In a large pot, mix together the fish bones, onion, celery, wine, parsley, lemon juice, water, and sea salt. Bring to a simmer over medium-low heat, skimming and discarding any foam from the surface.

2 Using a metal strainer, pour the mixture into a heat-proof container, pressing on the vegetables and fish pieces.

3 Use immediately or chill completely and then store in a covered container in the refrigerator for up to 2 days or in the freezer for up to 1 month.

COOKING TIP: Use mild fish and shellfish such as halibut, flounder, or shrimp shells to make this stock. Salmon, snapper, and deep-water fish will overpower the stock with an unpleasant flavor and oily texture.

Nutritional Information (1 cup) Calories: 64; Saturated Fat: 0g; Carbohydrates: 1g; Sodium: 109mg; Fiber: 0g; Protein: 4g

DASHI

YIELD 2 QUARTS **PREP** 30 MINS INACTIVE **COOK** 20 MINS

■ PALEO ■ GLUTEN-FREE

Dashi is a classic broth used in Japanese cuisine and serves as the base for miso soup. Kombu is edible kelp, and bonito flakes are very thin shavings of skipjack tuna that have been dried.

2 squares kombu
2½ quarts water
2 cups bonito flakes

1 In a large pot, combine the kombu and water. Allow to soak for 30 minutes. Turn the heat to medium-low and bring almost to a simmer for 5 minutes. Remove the kombu.

2 Increase the heat to medium-high and boil the broth for 5 minutes. Reduce the heat to low and add the bonito flakes. Cook at a low simmer for 10 minutes.

3 Using a fine-mesh strainer lined with cheesecloth, pour the broth into a heat-proof container.

4 Use immediately or chill completely and then store in a covered container in the refrigerator for up to 1 week or in the freezer for up to 1 month.

INGREDIENT TIP: These exotic-sounding ingredients are surprisingly easy to find in the Asian section of your local grocery store, at a specialty Asian market, or online.

Nutritional Information (1 cup) Calories: 11; Saturated Fat: 0g; Carbohydrates: 0g; Sodium: 37mg; Fiber: 0g; Protein: 2g

STOCKS, BROTHS & CLEAR SOUPS

MISO SOUP

SERVES 4 **PREP** 5 MINS **COOK** 5 MINS

■ GLUTEN-FREE ■ VEGAN

This soup is a comforting appetizer to enjoy before serving Cold Rice Noodle Salad with Sesame Vinaigrette (page 208) or your favorite sushi.

3 tablespoons white miso
1 quart dashi or water
8 ounces silken tofu, diced
2 scallions, thinly sliced on a bias
  for serving

1 In a small pot, bring the miso, dashi, and tofu to a simmer over medium heat.

2 Stir in the scallions and cook for 2 minutes.

3 Divide the soup among 4 serving bowls.

COOKING TIP: Do not cook the miso for longer than suggested. It begins to lose its flavor and nutrients during prolonged cooking.

Nutritional Information Calories: 63; Saturated Fat: 0g; Carbohydrates: 5g; Sodium: 502mg; Fiber: 1g; Protein: 6g

EGG DROP SOUP

SERVES 4 **PREP** 5 MINS **COOK** 10 MINS

■ PALEO-FRIENDLY ■ GLUTEN-FREE

This is a perfect light lunch or appetizer and oh-so-easy to make! I love how pretty the eggs are as they are swirled into the broth. There's so much to enjoy about the art of cooking.

1 tablespoon cornstarch
1 quart Chicken Broth
   (page 32), divided
1 teaspoon puréed fresh ginger
1 tablespoon soy sauce
2 scallions, sliced thinly on a bias
1 cup button mushrooms, sliced
Pinch white pepper
4 eggs, lightly beaten

1 In a small bowl, whisk the cornstarch with 3 or 4 tablespoons of the chicken broth.

2 In a large pot, combine the remaining chicken broth, ginger, soy sauce, scallions, and mushrooms. Season with the white pepper and bring the mixture to a simmer over medium heat.

3 Whisk in the cornstarch mixture and cook until just thickened.

4 Pour in the beaten eggs and swirl with a spoon or chopsticks until the eggs are cooked.

5 Remove the pot from the heat and serve immediately.

SUBSTITUTION TIP: Use gluten-free soy sauce to make this recipe gluten-free. To make it Paleo, use coconut aminos instead of soy sauce and use tapioca starch instead of cornstarch.

Nutritional Information Calories: 118; Saturated Fat: 2g; Carbohydrates: 5g; Sodium: 1054mg; Fiber: 0g; Protein: 11g

STOCKS, BROTHS & CLEAR SOUPS

3

CHILLED SOUPS

GAZPACHO

SERVES 4 TO 6 **PREP** 5 MINS **COOK** 0 MINS

■ PALEO ■ GLUTEN-FREE ■ VEGAN ■ BIG 8 ALLERGEN–FRIENDLY

My husband bought me a bottle of Cabernet vinegar in Madrid while on a photography assignment. I'm not sure how many wives would see vinegar as an exciting present, but I was thrilled! I crafted this gazpacho to showcase the vinegar and the heirloom tomatoes that were in season when he returned. The flavor of red wine vinegar is prominent in this recipe, so choose a high-quality vinegar if you can.

6 cups heirloom tomatoes, cored, divided
2 English cucumbers, divided
¼ cup red wine vinegar
¼ cup olive oil
Sea salt
Freshly ground black pepper
2 shallots, thinly sliced
6 basil leaves, thinly sliced

1 Roughly chop 4 cups of the tomatoes and place them in a blender. Peel one of the cucumbers, cut it into a few pieces, and add to the blender. Pour in the red wine vinegar and olive oil and season with salt and pepper. Purée until smooth.

2 Dice the remaining tomatoes and cucumber and toss them together with the shallots and basil leaves.

3 Divide the purée among individual serving bowls and place the diced cucumber and tomatoes in the center of each bowl. Serve immediately.

STORAGE TIP: Gazpacho is best enjoyed immediately, but leftovers may be stored separately in a covered container in the refrigerator for up to 2 days.

COOKING TIP: The flavor and texture of tomatoes deteriorate in the refrigerator, so always store them in a fruit basket or in a warm windowsill to ripen.

Nutritional Information Calories: 186; Saturated Fat: 2g; Carbohydrates: 17g; Sodium: 76mg; Fiber: 4g; Protein: 4g

SUMMER BERRIES IN AGRODOLCE

SERVES 4 TO 6 **PREP** 5 MINS **COOK** 10 MINS

▪ GLUTEN-FREE ▪ VEGAN ▪ BIG 8 ALLERGEN–FRIENDLY

I love the balance of sweet and sour flavors in this recipe. *Agrodolce* is a traditional sweet and sour sauce in Italian cuisine. It's lovely with berries here or drizzled over meats or salad.

½ cup sugar
½ cup red wine vinegar
2 cups blackberries
2 pints blueberries
2 pints raspberries
½ cup fresh mint leaves, roughly chopped

1 In a small pot over medium heat, cook the sugar, vinegar, and blackberries for 10 minutes, mashing the berries to release their juices. Press the mixture through a fine mesh sieve into a medium bowl to remove the blackberry seeds.

2 Divide the blueberries, raspberries, and mint among individual serving bowls. Drizzle with the agrodolce and toss gently to mix thoroughly. Allow to rest for 10 minutes at room temperature before serving.

3 The sauce may be stored in the refrigerator in a covered container for up to 1 week.

SUBSTITUTION TIP: Feel free to play around with this basic recipe, using different fruits and different kinds of vinegar. Sherry, balsamic, and apple cider vinegars are all lovely substitutes.

Nutritional Information Calories: 332; Saturated Fat: 0g; Carbohydrates: 43g; Sodium: 9mg; Fiber: 6g; Protein: 5g

VICHYSSOISE

SERVES 4 TO 6 **PREP** 10 MINS **COOK** 35 MINS

■ PALEO-FRIENDLY ■ GLUTEN-FREE ■ BIG 8 ALLERGEN–FRIENDLY

Unlike the preceding chilled soups, this one is cooked first and then cooled. It makes a perfect spring and early summer supper when chives are in season.

2 tablespoons unsalted butter
2 tablespoons olive oil
Sea salt
4 leeks, white and pale green parts only, thinly sliced
4 medium potatoes, peeled and diced
1 quart Chicken Broth (page 32) or Basic Vegetable Broth (page 28)
1 teaspoon white wine vinegar
½ cup heavy cream
⅛ teaspoon freshly ground nutmeg
¼ teaspoon white pepper
6 fresh chives, cut with kitchen shears, for serving

1 In a large pot, heat the butter and oil over medium-low heat. Add a generous pinch of sea salt and cook the leeks for 5 minutes.

2 Add the potatoes and cook for another 2 minutes. Pour in the chicken broth and bring to a simmer. Cover and cook for 30 minutes, until the vegetables are tender.

3 Add the vinegar and use an immersion blender to purée the soup.

4 Stir in the heavy cream, nutmeg, and white pepper and bring to a gentle simmer for 2 to 3 minutes. Adjust the seasonings.

5 Chill the soup thoroughly. When you're ready to serve, divide it among serving bowls and garnish with fresh chives.

6 Cover and store leftovers in the refrigerator for up to 4 days.

SUBSTITUTION TIP: To make this soup Paleo and vegan, replace the butter with olive oil, use vegetable broth, and replace the heavy cream with coconut cream.

Nutritional Information Calories: 405; Saturated Fat: 9g; Carbohydrates: 48g; Sodium: 899mg; Fiber: 7g; Protein: 10g

MACADAMIA NUT BISQUE

SERVES 4 TO 6 **PREP** 10 MINS **COOK** 0 MINS

■ PALEO ■ GLUTEN-FREE ■ VEGAN

One of the things I love about the raw vegan movement is that it's built around whole foods. Raw vegan recipes are full of flavor and offer a surprisingly wide array of textures. This simple creamy soup can be topped with anything you like, but I think it's perfect with just a drizzle of olive oil and a generous grind of black pepper.

2 cups raw, unsalted macadamia nuts, soaked for 1 hour
1 shallot, roughly chopped
2 garlic cloves, roughly chopped
1 teaspoon minced fresh rosemary
2 tablespoons white wine vinegar
2 to 3 cups water
¼ cup extra-virgin olive oil, plus 2 teaspoons for serving
Sea salt
Freshly ground black pepper
1 bunch fresh chives, roughly chopped, for serving

1 Rinse and drain the macadamia nuts, discarding the soaking water.

2 In a blender, mix together the macadamia nuts, shallot, garlic, rosemary, and white wine vinegar.

3 Pour in just enough water to cover the nuts by about 1 inch and blend until smooth. Add additional water to thin the soup to your desired consistency.

4 With the motor of the blender running, drizzle in ¼ cup of the olive oil. Season with salt and pepper and garnish with fresh chives and the remaining olive oil.

5 Chill thoroughly before serving. Store covered in the refrigerator for up to 2 days.

COOKING TIP: Leaving the motor of the blender running while you add the oil helps emulsify it, which means to disburse and suspend the oil droplets evenly throughout the soup.

Nutritional Information Calories: 606; Saturated Fat: 10g; Carbohydrates: 11g; Sodium: 63mg; Fiber: 6g; Protein: 6g

AVOCADO BASIL SOUP

SERVES 4 TO 6 **PREP** 10 MINS **COOK** 0 MINS

■ PALEO ■ GLUTEN-FREE ■ VEGAN ■ BIG 8 ALLERGEN–FRIENDLY

This is the perfect appetizer soup for summer when fresh basil abounds. If you're using organic cucumber, you do not need to peel it. The color of the soup will be a little greener and it will have a slightly coarser texture, but it will offer greater nutrient density.

2 ripe avocadoes, pitted and peeled
1 cucumber, peeled and seeded
2 celery stalks, diced
1 to 2 cups water
1 teaspoon white wine vinegar
1 cup fresh basil leaves, plus more
  for serving
¼ cup plus 2 teaspoons extra-virgin
  olive oil, divided
Sea salt
Freshly ground black pepper

1 In a blender, combine the avocado, cucumber, celery, 1 cup of water, vinegar, and basil. Purée until smooth. Add water until you achieve the desired consistency.

2 With the motor of the blender still running, pour in the ¼ cup of olive oil. Season with salt.

3 To serve, ladle the soup into individual serving bowls and drizzle the remaining olive oil over top. Season with freshly ground black pepper and garnish each serving with a fresh basil leaf.

4 This soup is best enjoyed right away because the avocado begins to discolor immediately after being cut. However, if you wish, you can cover and store leftovers in the refrigerator for up to 2 days.

SUBSTITUTION TIP: You could substitute any fresh delicate herb you like in this soup. It's lovely with cilantro and a squeeze of lime juice as well, and reminds me of a creamy guacamole.

Nutritional Information Calories: 347; Saturated Fat: 6g; Carbohydrates: 12g; Sodium: 73mg; Fiber: 7g; Protein: 3g

WHITE GAZPACHO

SERVES 4 TO 6 **PREP** 15 MINS **COOK** 0 MINS

■ PALEO-FRIENDLY ■ GLUTEN-FREE ■ VEGAN

When I think of gazpacho, my mind immediately races to tomatoes, vinegar, and cucumber. But there's another side to this cold summertime soup, and it's sweet, savory, creamy, and delicious. It's best enjoyed with a cold glass of dry Spanish sherry.

4 cups peeled and diced cucumber, divided

3 cups halved green grapes, divided

1¼ cups slivered almonds, divided

2 slices white bread or gluten-free bread, crusts removed

4 garlic cloves, minced

¼ cup extra-virgin olive oil

4 tablespoons red wine vinegar

1 cup water

Sea salt

Freshly ground black pepper

2 scallions, sliced thinly on a bias, for serving

1 In a blender, mix together 3½ cups of the cucumber, 2½ cups of the grapes, 1 cup of the almonds, the bread, garlic, oil, vinegar, and water. Purée until smooth, adding more water as needed to achieve desired consistency.

2 Season with salt and pepper. For a smooth, thin soup, pass it through a metal strainer or china cap. Chill thoroughly before serving.

3 To serve, ladle the soup into individual serving bowls. Top with the remaining ½ cup of diced cucumber, ½ cup of grapes, ¼ cup of slivered almonds, and scallions.

4 Cover and refrigerate the soup and garnishes separately for up to 2 days.

COOKING TIP: Make this soup ahead of time and pack it for a filling vegan lunch during the summer months. You'll look forward to it all morning! To make it Paleo, simply omit the bread and do not strain the soup to keep it nice and thick.

Nutritional Information Calories: 360; Saturated Fat: 3g; Carbohydrates: 26g; Sodium: 94mg; Fiber: 5g; Protein: 8g

MINT & PEA SOUP

SERVES 4 TO 6 **PREP** 10 MINS **COOK** 0 MINS

■ PALEO ■ GLUTEN-FREE ■ VEGAN ■ BIG 8 ALLERGEN–FRIENDLY

I tried to embrace all of the new foods available while we lived in England, even mushy peas. Think "mashed potatoes meet peas" and you have a good idea of their consistency. Perhaps the idea for mushy peas was conceived by a parent who was tired of peas rolling off their children's plates. Whatever the origin, they're especially delicious with fresh mint.

2 cups fresh shelled or frozen and
    defrosted peas
2 mint sprigs, leaves only, plus more
    for garnish
2 fresh chives
2 cups Basic Vegetable Broth (page 28)
1 tablespoon white wine vinegar
¼ cup extra-virgin olive oil
Sea salt
Freshly ground black pepper

1 In a blender, mix together the peas, mint, chives, broth, and vinegar. Purée until smooth.

2 With the motor of the blender still running, pour in the olive oil. Season with salt and pepper.

3 Serve immediately or store covered in the refrigerator for up to 3 days.

INGREDIENT TIP: Technically, peas belong to the legume family and are therefore not strict Paleo. However, many experts in Paleo nutrition make an exception for peas and green beans.

Nutritional Information Calories: 187; Saturated Fat: 2g; Carbohydrates: 11g; Sodium: 157mg; Fiber: 4g; Protein: 6g

CHICKPEA PARSLEY SOUP

SERVES 4 TO 6 **PREP** 10 MINS **COOK** 0 MINS

■ GLUTEN-FREE ■ VEGAN ■ BIG 8 ALLERGEN–FRIENDLY

The flavors of the Middle East permeate this creamy vegan soup. If you cannot find tahini, feel free to use 2 tablespoons of toasted sesame oil instead.

2 cups canned chickpeas

1 cup fresh parsley leaves, plus more for serving

2 garlic cloves

¼ cup fresh lemon juice

¼ cup tahini

1 teaspoon ground coriander

1 teaspoon ground cumin

2 to 3 cups water

¼ cup olive oil

Sea salt

Freshly ground black pepper

1 cup halved grape tomatoes, for serving

¼ cup toasted pine nuts, for serving

1 teaspoon smoked paprika, for serving

1 In a blender, mix together the chickpeas, parsley, garlic, lemon juice, tahini, coriander, cumin, and 1 cup of water. Purée until smooth, and add more water to achieve the desired consistency.

2 With the motor of the blender still running, drizzle in the olive oil. Season with salt and pepper.

3 To serve, ladle the soup into individual serving bowls and top each serving with additional parsley, tomatoes, pine nuts, and a pinch of smoked paprika.

COOKING TIP: To accommodate for nut allergies, skip the pine nuts. To toast pine nuts, heat a dry skillet over medium heat and shake the pine nuts back and forth in the skillet until lightly browned and fragrant.

Nutritional Information Calories: 413; Saturated Fat: 5g; Carbohydrates: 29g; Sodium: 103mg; Fiber: 9g; Protein: 13g

SALMOREJO SPANISH BREAD & TOMATO SOUP

SERVES 4 TO 6 **PREP** 20 MINS **COOK** 0 MINS

■ GLUTEN-FREE ■ VEGAN

This creamy tomato soup originated in southern Spain, where it is served with serrano ham and hard-boiled eggs. It's also delicious with roughly chopped roasted almonds and a drizzle of coconut cream if you want a vegan version.

4 slices white bread, crusts removed
4 pounds fresh tomatoes
4 garlic cloves
2 tablespoons sherry vinegar
2 tablespoons olive oil
Sea salt
Freshly ground black pepper
2 hard-boiled eggs, chopped, for serving
2 ounces diced serrano ham, for serving

1 Soak the bread in a medium bowl of water. Set aside.

2 Bring 2 quarts of water to a boil in a large pot. Plunge the tomatoes into the water for 1 minute, then remove to a large bowl of ice water. Remove the tomato skins, cores, and seeds. Don't worry if you cannot get them all.

3 In a blender, purée the tomatoes with the garlic, vinegar, and olive oil.

4 Wring the excess moisture from the bread and add it to the blender in three separate batches, blending for 5 seconds in between.

5 Season with salt and pepper.

6 Chill completely. Serve with the hard-boiled eggs and serrano ham.

SUBSTITUTION TIP: Feel free to use gluten-free bread in this recipe.

Nutritional Information Calories: 267; Saturated Fat: 2g; Carbohydrates: 32g; Sodium: 498mg; Fiber: 5g; Protein: 11g

STRAWBERRY GAZPACHO

SERVES 4 TO 6 **PREP** 10 MINS **COOK** 0 MINS

■ PALEO ■ GLUTEN-FREE ■ VEGAN ■ BIG 8 ALLERGEN–FRIENDLY

I remember picking strawberries as a child, their sweet juices dripping down my hands and face as I ate just as many as I plopped into my basket. The flavor is a distant memory when I bite into most conventionally grown strawberries from the grocery store. But when I visit the farmers' market, strawberries taste like they're supposed to taste. Save this dessert soup for the peak of strawberry season and purchase them from a farmers' market or pick them yourself for the best flavor.

4 cups hulled and halved
    fresh strawberries
1 teaspoon granulated sugar
1 tablespoon balsamic vinegar
2 cups diced fresh tomatoes
1 cucumber, peeled and seeded
1 shallot, minced
4 tablespoons extra-virgin olive
    oil, divided
Sea salt
Freshly ground black pepper
¼ cup fresh flat-leaf parsley leaves,
    for serving

1 In a large bowl, mix the strawberries with the sugar and balsamic vinegar and allow the fruit to soften and release its liquid for 1 hour at room temperature.

2 Transfer the marinated strawberries and their juices to a blender, along with the tomatoes, cucumber, shallot, and 3 tablespoons of the olive oil. Purée until smooth. Season with salt and pepper.

3 Serve with a generous grind of pepper, parsley, and the remaining 1 tablespoon of olive oil drizzled over the top.

4 Serve immediately or cover and store leftovers in the refrigerator for up to 2 days.

INGREDIENT TIP: Summer fruits such as tomatoes and strawberries taste best when they're bursting with the goodness of the sunshine, so don't put this soup in the refrigerator unless you absolutely have to.

Nutritional Information Calories: 201; Saturated Fat: 2g; Carbohydrates: 19g; Sodium: 68mg; Fiber: 5g; Protein: 2g

CUCUMBER MELON SOUP

SERVES 4 TO 6 **PREP** 10 MINS **COOK** 0 MINS

■ PALEO ■ GLUTEN-FREE ■ VEGAN ■ BIG 8 ALLERGEN–FRIENDLY

Ripe melons and cucumbers beg to be blended into a chilled soup and enjoyed on a hot summer afternoon. This soup can be served as either an appetizer or dessert. If you want to serve it for dessert, simply skip the garnish or pour the puréed soup into an ice cream maker for a light and refreshing sorbet.

2 cucumbers, peeled, seeded, and cut into 1-inch chunks

1 ripe honeydew melon, peeled, seeded, and cut into 1-inch chunks

¼ cup minced fresh cilantro

1 tablespoon minced fresh mint

1 tablespoon fresh lemon juice

Sea salt

1 Chop ½ cup of the cucumber and ½ cup of the melon into very small dice and transfer them to a medium bowl. Add the cilantro and mint and toss well.

2 Place the remaining cucumber and melon in a blender along with the lemon juice and a small pinch of sea salt. Purée until smooth.

3 Pour the soup into individual serving bowls and top each serving with some of the chopped cucumber-melon garnish.

4 Serve immediately or cover and store in the refrigerator for up to 2 days.

INGREDIENT TIP: If you have access to a good farmers' market, look for lemon basil. Add ¼ cup of the leaves to this soup and use a few leaves for garnish in place of the cilantro and mint.

Nutritional Information Calories: 140; Saturated Fat: 0g; Carbohydrates: 35g; Sodium: 62mg; Fiber: 4g; Protein: 3g

COLD PEACH SOUP

SERVES 4 TO 6 **PREP** 10 MINS **COOK** 0 MINS

■ PALEO-FRIENDLY ■ GLUTEN-FREE ■ VEGETARIAN ■ BIG 8 ALLERGEN–FRIENDLY

I finally watched the movie *Endless Summer* while writing this book, and I love the idea of basking in the sun all year round. If you're making this soup in the summertime, use fresh peaches. To create an endless summer in the middle of winter, defrost frozen peaches and use them instead. Prefer a really cold soup? Pour this into an ice cream maker and process until it reaches a thick, soft-serve consistency.

6 cups peeled, diced fresh peaches, from about 8 whole peaches
1 teaspoon apple cider vinegar
1 teaspoon vanilla extract
1 cup plain whole-milk Greek yogurt
Pinch sea salt
Toasted sliced almonds, for serving (optional)
¼ cup balsamic vinegar reduction, for serving (optional)

1 In a food processor, purée the peaches, vinegar, and vanilla until smooth.

2 Add the yogurt and sea salt and pulse until they are fully incorporated.

3 Serve with toasted almonds and balsamic reduction (if using). Cover and store leftovers in the refrigerator for up to 2 days.

SUBSTITUTION TIP: To make this Paleo and dairy-free, use a coconut yogurt or coconut cream in place of the Greek yogurt.

INGREDIENT TIP: You can find balsamic reduction at a specialty market or make your own by cooking 1 cup of balsamic vinegar over low heat until it is reduced to ¼ cup, about 15 minutes. Be careful to keep it just below a simmer so as not to scorch it.

Nutritional Information Calories: 135; Saturated Fat: 2g; Carbohydrates: 22g; Sodium: 84mg; Fiber: 3g; Protein: 7g

VANILLA CANTALOUPE SOUP

SERVES 4 TO 6 **PREP** 10 MINS **COOK** 0 MINS

■ PALEO-FRIENDLY ■ GLUTEN-FREE ■ VEGAN ■ BIG 8 ALLERGEN–FRIENDLY

I first tried cantaloupe with vanilla bean when making jam from the cookbook *Food in Jars*, and the flavors were mind-blowing. It was seriously delicious—so good that I could never get enough into the jam jars to can it. Like the other fruit soups in this chapter, feel free to pour it into your ice cream maker to make a delicious sorbet. If you're feeling really festive, I won't tell anyone if you add ½ cup dark rum as well. Just don't serve it to the kids!

1 cantaloupe melon, peeled, seeded, and diced
Seeds from 1 vanilla bean
1 tablespoon fresh lemon juice
¼ cup packed brown sugar
Pinch sea salt

1 In a blender, mix together the melon, vanilla bean seeds, lemon juice, brown sugar, and sea salt. Purée until smooth.

2 Chill for at least 1 hour to allow the flavors to meld thoroughly.

3 Cover and store leftovers in the refrigerator for up to 2 days.

SUBSTITUTION TIP: To make this Paleo, use maple syrup instead of brown sugar. If you don't want to purchase a whole vanilla bean, feel free to use 1 tablespoon of vanilla extract instead.

Nutritional Information Calories: 47; Saturated Fat: 0g; Carbohydrates: 12g; Sodium: 67mg; Fiber: 0g; Protein: 0g

SOUP & COMFORT

TIRAMISU SOUP

SERVES 4 TO 6 **PREP** 10 MINS, PLUS 1 HOUR SOAKING TIME **COOK** 0 MINS

■ PALEO ■ GLUTEN-FREE ■ VEGAN

The flavors of this classic Italian dessert get a raw, vegan makeover in this chilled soup. Unlike the original, it's naturally free of dairy, eggs, and wheat (not to mention the risk of salmonella from consuming raw eggs). Feel free to use cashews in place of the macadamia nuts if you wish.

1 cup macadamia nuts, soaked in water for 1 hour
1 cup medjool dates, pitted and soaked in 1 cup of water for 1 hour
1 ounce espresso or very strong brewed coffee
2 ounces dark rum
1 tablespoon vanilla extract
Pinch sea salt
1 to 2 cups water
¼ cup coconut oil
½ cup chocolate shavings, for serving

1 Rinse and drain the macadamia nuts.

2 In a blender, mix the macadamia nuts with the dates and their soaking liquid. Pour in the espresso, rum, vanilla, salt, and 1 cup of water.

3 Purée until very smooth. Add more water until the soup reaches the desired consistency.

4 With the motor of the blender still running, drizzle in the coconut oil and blend for 10 seconds.

5 Refrigerate the soup until it is completely chilled, then pour it into individual serving bowls or cups. Garnish with chocolate shavings.

6 Cover and store leftovers in the refrigerator for up to 2 days.

COOKING TIP: Make sure to soak the macadamia nuts or cashews and dates separately; the cashew soaking water should be discarded, whereas the sweet date water will go into the purée.

Nutritional Information Calories: 511; Saturated Fat: 18g; Carbohydrates: 26g; Sodium: 62mg; Fiber: 5g; Protein: 4g

AVOCADO BISQUE
WITH ORANGE PEPPER SALAD

SERVES 4 TO 6 **PREP** 10 MINS **COOK** 0 MINS

■ PALEO ■ GLUTEN-FREE ■ VEGAN ■ BIG 8 ALLERGEN–FRIENDLY

My mom says that avocados were my favorite food as a baby. It's not surprising then that I still enjoy them plain or with just a pinch of salt and a sprinkle of vinegar. This soup preserves the delicate flavor and creaminess of avocado and complements it with grassy cucumber and sweet orange. It rivals guacamole as one of my favorite ways to enjoy avocado. Although this soup is best enjoyed immediately, you can store leftovers separately in a covered container in the refrigerator for up to 1 day.

1 orange
1 English cucumber, roughly chopped
3 ripe avocados, pitted and peeled
1 quart water
1 celery stalk, diced
Juice of 2 limes, divided
1 cup roughly chopped fresh cilantro, divided
1 teaspoon ground coriander
1 teaspoon sea salt
1 red bell pepper, finely diced

1 Zest the orange. Slice off the top and bottom of the fruit and remove the peel. Use a paring knife to remove each segment of fruit from between the membranes and set aside.

2 In a blender, combine the orange zest, cucumber, avocado, water, celery, half of the lime juice, ½ cup of cilantro, coriander, and sea salt. Purée until smooth.

3 Add the red bell pepper and the remaining ½ cup of cilantro and lime juice to the orange segments and toss gently to mix. Chill thoroughly.

4 Divide the avocado purée among individual serving bowls and place the orange and bell pepper salad in the center of each bowl. Serve immediately.

INGREDIENT TIP: Keep cilantro fresh in your refrigerator by placing the stems in a glass of water and covering the leaves with a loose plastic bag.

Nutritional Information Calories: 363; Saturated Fat: 6g; Carbohydrates: 27g; Sodium: 490mg; Fiber: 14g; Protein: 5g

4

PURÉED SOUPS

CURRIED SWEET POTATO SOUP

SERVES 4 TO 6 **PREP** 5 MINS **COOK** 30 MINS

■ PALEO-FRIENDLY ■ GLUTEN-FREE ■ VEGAN ■ FIX-AND-FORGET

After trying several versions, I fell in love with sweet potato soup when I made this sweet and spicy vegan version. It's big on flavor with a comforting, creamy texture. For a little crunch, top it with crushed toasted almonds. Serve with a loaf of crusty bread.

1 quart Roasted Vegetable Broth (page 29)
2 large sweet potatoes, peeled and diced, about 4 cups total
1 yellow onion, diced
2 garlic cloves, smashed
1 (¼-inch) slice peeled fresh ginger
¼ teaspoon red chili flakes
1 cup coconut milk
2 tablespoons curry powder
1 teaspoon packed brown sugar
1 teaspoon garam masala
1 teaspoon fresh lime juice
Sea salt

1 In a large pot, mix together the broth, sweet potatoes, onion, garlic, ginger, and red chili flakes and bring to a simmer over medium heat. Cover and cook for about 20 minutes, or until the vegetables are tender.

2 Remove the ginger and stir in the coconut milk, curry powder, and brown sugar. Simmer uncovered for 5 minutes.

3 Stir in the garam masala and lime juice.

4 Use an immersion blender to purée the soup until completely smooth. To avoid splattering, be careful not to lift the blender out of the pot.

5 Season with salt. Serve immediately.

6 Store cooled leftovers in a covered container in the refrigerator for up to 2 days.

FIX-AND-FORGET: To make this soup in a slow cooker, simply place all of the ingredients except the lime juice in a 4-quart slow cooker and cook on low for 6 hours or on high for 3 hours. For an optional extra step, you can stir in the lime juice at the very end, after the soup is cooked.

SUBSTITUTION TIP: If you prefer not to make the Roasted Vegetable Broth, use a store-bought chicken broth instead. To make the recipe Paleo, replace the brown sugar with maple syrup.

Nutritional Information Calories: 340; Saturated Fat: 16g; Carbohydrates: 43g; Sodium: 845mg; Fiber: 8g; Protein: 9g

CREAMY TOMATO SOUP

SERVES 4 TO 6 **PREP** 5 MINS **COOK** 25 MINS

■ GLUTEN-FREE

The idea of tomato soup takes me straight back to second grade, track and field days, and grilled cheese sandwiches. This version has received a grown-up upgrade, but it's just as good with its trusty sidekick, Gourmet Grilled Cheese (page 217). To make a chiffonade with the basil, stack the leaves on top of one another and roll them into a tight cylinder. Use a sharp chef's knife to make perpendicular cuts to produce thin circles of basil.

4 tablespoons extra-virgin olive oil, divided
4 shallots, minced
2 garlic cloves, minced
Pinch red chili flakes
Sea salt
1 (28-ounce) can whole peeled tomatoes, hand crushed
2 cups Chicken Broth (page 32) or Parmesan Broth (page 30)
½ cup heavy cream, divided
6 fresh basil leaves, for serving (optional)

1 In a large pot, heat 2 tablespoons of the oil over medium-low heat and cook the shallots, garlic, and red chili flakes with a generous pinch of salt for 10 minutes, until soft.

2 Increase the heat to medium and add the tomatoes and their juices. Pour in the broth and bring to a gentle simmer for 10 minutes.

3 Remove the pot from the heat and allow to cool for 5 minutes. Use an immersion blender to purée the soup, or pass it through a china cap.

4 Whisk in ⅓ cup of the heavy cream. Season with salt.

5 To serve, divide soup among individual serving bowls and drizzle with the remaining heavy cream and olive oil. Garnish each bowl with a chiffonade of fresh basil (if using).

6 Store cooled leftovers in a covered container in the refrigerator for up to 3 days.

Nutritional Information Calories: 246; Saturated Fat: 6g; Carbohydrates: 13g; Sodium: 473mg; Fiber: 2g; Protein: 6g

SMOKY ROASTED CORN & TOMATO SOUP

SERVES 4 TO 6 **PREP** 15 MINS **COOK** 20 MINS

■ PALEO ■ GLUTEN-FREE ■ BIG 8 ALLERGEN–FRIENDLY

My mom gave me the recipe for this smoky, delicious summer soup from a farm-to-table dinner in southwestern Washington. It was a benefit event to support the firefighters battling record wildfires that year. Despite the challenging circumstances, the food brought friends and neighbors together.

4 pounds halved fresh tomatoes

4 cups fresh corn kernels, divided

2 tablespoons olive oil

6 slices applewood-smoked bacon, roughly chopped

1 onion, diced

4 garlic cloves, minced

1 quart Roasted Chicken Stock (page 31)

1 teaspoon smoked paprika

1 teaspoon ancho chili powder

Sea salt

Freshly ground black pepper

1 teaspoon apple cider vinegar

1 cup roughly chopped fresh cilantro, for serving

1 Preheat the broiler.

2 On a sheet pan, spread out the tomatoes and 3½ cups of the corn and drizzle with the olive oil. Broil for 3 to 5 minutes, until the vegetables are lightly charred.

3 In a large pot, cook the bacon over medium-low heat until cooked through, 10 to 12 minutes. To keep as much bacon fat in the pan as possible, remove the bacon with a slotted spoon and set aside.

4 Cook the onion in the bacon fat for 5 minutes, until it begins to soften. Add the garlic and cook for 30 seconds.

5 Add the chicken stock, paprika, chili powder, roasted corn, and tomatoes. Season with salt and pepper. Bring to a simmer and cook, uncovered, for 20 minutes.

6 Stir in the vinegar and then purée the soup with an immersion blender until smooth.

7 To serve, ladle the soup into individual serving bowls. Top with the remaining ½ cup of fresh corn kernels, the cooked bacon, and cilantro.

SUBSTITUTION TIP: If you're making this soup in the dead of winter but want the flavors of summer, purchase two 15-ounce cans of whole fire-roasted tomatoes and two 16-ounce bags of frozen charred corn kernels.

Nutritional Information Calories: 345; Saturated Fat: 3g; Carbohydrates: 51g; Sodium: 1057mg; Fiber: 9g; Protein: 14g

PURÉED SOUPS

PUMPKIN SOUP

SERVES 4 TO 6 **PREP** 10 MINS **COOK** 20 MINS

■ PALEO ■ GLUTEN-FREE ■ VEGAN ■ BIG 8 ALLERGEN–FRIENDLY ■ FIX-AND-FORGET

The flavors of Thanksgiving are so comforting to me, especially the cubed bread dressing seasoned with sage and celery, which typically accompanies turkey. This pumpkin soup captures those flavors so you can celebrate with gratitude all season long. If you cannot find fresh pumpkin, use butternut squash instead.

6 cups diced fresh pumpkin
1 onion, diced
2 celery stalks, diced
2 garlic cloves, minced
1 thyme sprig
1 sage sprig
Sea salt
1 quart Chicken Broth (page 32)
Toasted pumpkin seeds, for serving
  (optional)

FIX-AND-FORGET: Place all of the ingredients in a 4-quart slow cooker and cook on low for 6 hours or on high for 2 hours.

1 In a large pot, mix together the pumpkin, onion, celery, garlic, thyme, and sage. Season with salt. Pour in the chicken broth and bring to a simmer for 20 to 25 minutes, or until the pumpkin is soft.

2 Remove the herb sprigs and then purée the soup with an immersion blender until smooth.

3 Ladle into individual serving bowls and top with toasted pumpkin seeds (if using).

4 Store cooled leftovers in a covered container in the refrigerator for up to 3 days.

PREPARATION TIP: For a fun presentation, serve this soup in hollowed-out miniature pumpkins and garnish with fresh minced sage.

Nutritional Information Calories: 179; Saturated Fat: 1g; Carbohydrates: 34g; Sodium: 790mg; Fiber: 12g; Protein: 9g

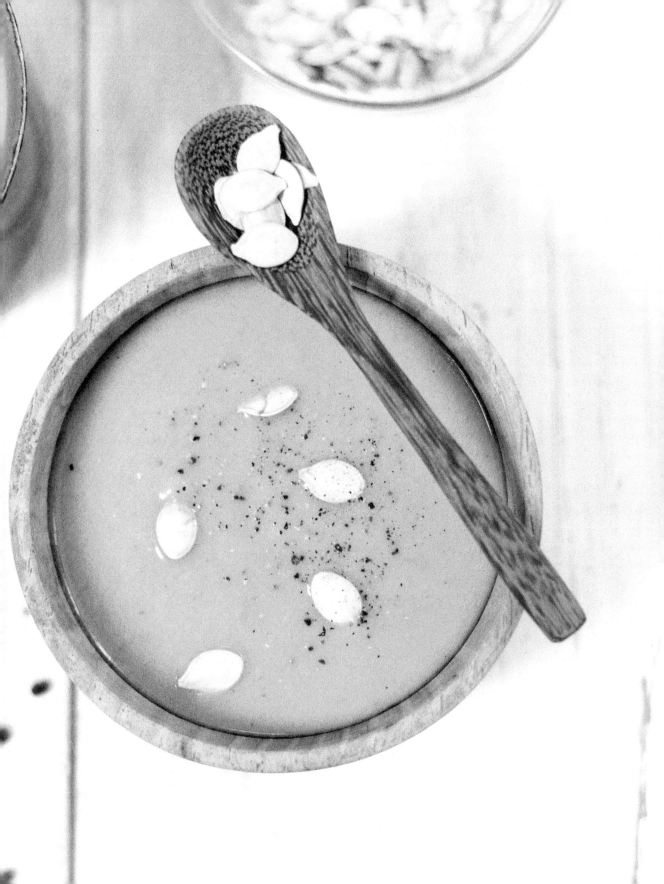

ROASTED BUTTERNUT SQUASH SOUP WITH SAGE

SERVES 4 TO 6 **PREP** 10 MINS **COOK** 50 MINS

■ PALEO-FRIENDLY ■ GLUTEN-FREE

Roasting vegetables brings out their natural sweetness. This soup reminds me of breakfasts as a kid when my mom would roast acorn squash and top it with brown sugar and butter. It wasn't exactly dessert, but it sure tasted like it.

6 cups cubed butternut squash
2 tablespoons olive oil
2 tablespoons melted unsalted butter
1 teaspoon ground cinnamon
⅛ teaspoon allspice
Sea salt
1 quart Chicken Broth (page 32)
1 teaspoon apple cider vinegar
1 teaspoon packed brown sugar
Leaves from 1 sage sprig, minced

1 Preheat the oven to 375°F.

2 Line a sheet pan with parchment paper. Spread the butternut squash out on the sheet pan and drizzle with the oil and butter. Season with the cinnamon, allspice, and a generous pinch of salt. Roast uncovered for 40 to 45 minutes, or until the squash is just beginning to brown.

3 Remove the squash from the oven and transfer it to a large pot. Pour in the chicken broth, bring it to a simmer over medium heat, and cook for 5 minutes to heat through. Add the vinegar and sugar and purée with an immersion blender until smooth. Season with salt and stir in the fresh sage.

4 Store cooled leftovers in a covered container in the refrigerator for up to 3 days.

SUBSTITUTION TIP: To make this Paleo, replace the melted butter with coconut oil and the brown sugar with maple syrup. To make it vegan, simply replace the chicken broth with Basic Vegetable Broth (page 28).

Nutritional Information Calories: 214; Saturated Fat: 5g; Carbohydrates: 17g; Sodium: 863mg; Fiber: 3g; Protein: 6g

SOUP & COMFORT

68

CREAM OF MUSHROOM SOUP

SERVES 4 TO 6 **PREP** 10 MINS **COOK** 15 MINS

■ VEGETARIAN

If a can of gelatinous glop comes to mind when you think of cream of mushroom soup, I feel your pain. Nearly every mid-century casserole recipe began with a can of cream of mushroom. But real cream of mushroom soup bursts with earthy umami flavors in a comforting vegetarian cream.

4 tablespoons unsalted butter, divided
2 cups sliced mushrooms
Sea salt
2 tablespoons all-purpose flour
*1½ quarts Roasted Vegetable Broth
    (page 29), heated*
2 tablespoons sherry
½ cup heavy cream
2 egg yolks
Freshly ground black pepper

1 Melt 2 tablespoons of the butter in a large skillet over medium-high heat, add the mushrooms, and cook until they are tender and golden brown, about 1 to 2 minutes on each side. Season with salt and set aside.

2 In a large pot over medium heat, melt the remaining 2 tablespoons of butter and whisk in the flour. Whisk in the vegetable broth and sherry. Bring to a simmer for 2 minutes until thickened.

3 In a large mixing bowl, whisk together the heavy cream and egg yolks. Slowly whisk in 1 cup of the thickened broth and then the remaining broth. Return to the pot, add the cooked mushrooms, and cook for 2 minutes until thick. Season with salt and pepper.

4 Serve immediately or chill, cover, and refrigerate for up to 2 days. Reheat slowly over low heat.

Nutritional Information Calories: 250; Saturated Fat: 12g; Carbohydrates: 6g; Sodium: 534mg; Fiber: 0g; Protein: 6g

CREAMY CAULIFLOWER PARMESAN SOUP

SERVES 4 TO 6 **PREP** 5 MINS **COOK** 35 MINS

■ GLUTEN-FREE ■ VEGETARIAN

Cauliflower provides a delicious, creamy base for this soup with negligible calories and carbohydrates. Use a micro-plane grater to create fluffy shavings of Parmesan. They will dissolve easily into the soup.

1 cauliflower head, broken into florets
4 garlic cloves
1½ quarts Parmesan Broth (page 30)
1 teaspoon white wine vinegar
¼ cup heavy cream
4 ounces Parmesan cheese, grated
Sea salt

1 In a large pot, mix together the cauliflower, garlic, and broth. Simmer for 25 minutes, until the cauliflower is tender.

2 Add the white wine vinegar and purée with an immersion blender until smooth. Allow to cool for 5 minutes.

3 Stir in the heavy cream and Parmesan and cook over low heat until the cheese is melted. Season with salt.

4 Store cooled leftovers in a covered container in the refrigerator for up to 3 days.

COOKING TIP: For a crunchy topping, make Parmesan crisps by baking small piles of shaved Parmesan on parchment paper at 350°F until browned. Allow to cool on a rack before serving.

Nutritional Information Calories: 161; Saturated Fat: 7g; Carbohydrates: 6g; Sodium: 411mg; Fiber: 2g; Protein: 13g

ASIAGO BISQUE

SERVES 4 TO 6 **PREP** 10 MINS **COOK** 30 MINS

■ GLUTEN-FREE ■ VEGETARIAN

This soup is a dairy-lover's dream. Asiago has a deliciously sweet, nutty flavor, which is accentuated by roasted garlic in this creamy, comforting soup. It's amazing with several homemade croutons scattered on top. Pair it with a crisp white wine to cut some of the fat.

2 tablespoons unsalted butter
1 leek, white and pale green parts only, thinly sliced
1 celery stalk, diced
1 carrot, diced
Sea salt
1 head roasted garlic
4 Yukon Gold potatoes, peeled and diced
1½ quarts Basic Vegetable Broth (page 28) or Chicken Broth (page 32)
1 teaspoon white wine vinegar
¼ cup heavy cream
8 ounces Asiago cheese, grated

1 In a large pot over medium-low heat, mix together the butter, leek, celery, and carrot. Season generously with salt. Cook for 10 minutes, until the vegetables have softened.

2 Add the garlic, potatoes, and broth. Bring to a simmer and cook for 20 minutes, until the potatoes are soft. Add the vinegar and purée with an immersion blender. Remove from the heat and cool slightly. Stir in the heavy cream and Asiago cheese. Cook over low heat until the cheese is melted. Serve immediately.

3 Store cooled leftovers in a covered container in the refrigerator for up to 3 days.

SUBSTITUTION TIP: Feel free to substitute another hard cheese, such as Parmesan, for the Asiago.

Nutritional Information Calories: 500; Saturated Fat: 16g; Carbohydrates: 40g; Sodium: 1973mg; Fiber: 3g; Protein: 26g

PURÉED SOUPS

SHARP CHEDDAR BISQUE

SERVES 4 TO 6 **PREP** 10 MINS **COOK** 25 MINS

■ PALEO ■ GLUTEN-FREE ■ VEGETARIAN

I grew up within driving distance of Tillamook Creamery and enjoyed their Cheddar cheese best of all. As I got older, I came to appreciate the sharp Cheddar especially. It shines in this soup and goes well with sliced scallions.

2 tablespoons unsalted butter
1 onion, diced
2 garlic cloves, minced
2 tablespoons all-purpose flour
1½ quarts chicken or vegetable broth
1 teaspoon white wine vinegar
2 cups whole milk
16 ounces sharp Cheddar cheese, grated, plus more for serving
2 scallions, thinly sliced on a bias

1 Melt the butter in a large pot over medium-high heat and cook the onion and garlic for 5 minutes or until the onion is soft and translucent. Sprinkle in the flour and cook for 2 minutes, stirring constantly. Pour in the broth and simmer, uncovered, for 10 minutes.

2 Add the vinegar and purée the soup with an immersion blender.

3 Remove the pot from the heat and allow the soup to cool for 5 minutes.

4 Stir in the milk and grated cheese. Cook over low heat until the cheese is melted.

5 Ladle the soup into individual serving bowls and garnish with scallions and additional cheese.

6 Store cooled leftovers in a covered container in the refrigerator for up to 3 days.

PAIRING TIP: Serve with French bread.

Nutritional Information Calories: 657; Saturated Fat: 30g; Carbohydrates: 15g; Sodium: 1950mg; Fiber: 1g; Protein: 41g

SOUP & COMFORT

PARSNIP SOUP

SERVES 4 TO 6 **PREP** 10 MINS **COOK** 25 MINS

■ GLUTEN-FREE ■ VEGETARIAN ■ FIX-AND-FORGET

Parsnips resemble ivory-colored carrots and have a sweet flavor and creamy texture. They're best in the late fall and early winter after the first frost. The cooler temperatures help the vegetable convert its starches into sugars. For a beautiful presentation and a nice contrast of texture and flavor, top the soup with roasted parsnips (see cooking tip).

6 to 8 parsnips, cut into 1-inch pieces
2 garlic cloves, smashed
1 shallot, quartered
1 quart Chicken Broth (page 32) or Basic
   Vegetable Broth (page 28)
1 thyme sprig
1 teaspoon white wine vinegar
¼ cup heavy cream
Sea salt
White pepper

 FIX-AND-FORGET: To make this soup in a slow cooker, simply place all of the ingredients except the heavy cream in a 4-quart slow cooker and cook on low for 4 hours or on high for 2 hours. For an optional extra step, you can stir in the heavy cream at the very end, after the soup is cooked.

1 In a large pot, mix together the parsnips, garlic, shallot, chicken broth, and thyme sprig over medium heat. Bring the broth to a simmer, cover the pot, and cook for 25 minutes or until the parsnips are tender.

2 Remove the thyme sprig, stir in the vinegar, and purée the soup with an immersion blender. For an extra smooth soup, pass it through a china cap.

3 Whisk in the heavy cream. Season with salt and white pepper. Cook for 5 minutes over medium-low to meld the flavors.

4 Store cooled leftovers in a covered container in the refrigerator for up to 3 days.

COOKING TIP: To prepare roasted parsnips, preheat the oven to 400°F. Chop parsnips into ½-inch pieces, season with olive oil, salt, and pepper, and spread out on a sheet pan. Roast uncovered for 25 to 30 minutes, until lightly browned and caramelized.

Nutritional Information Calories: 249; Saturated Fat: 2g; Carbohydrates: 50g; Sodium: 470mg; Fiber: 13g; Protein: 6g

PUREED SOUPS

CREAM OF WATERCRESS SOUP

SERVES 4 TO 6 **PREP** 10 MINS **COOK** 15 MINS

■ PALEO-FRIENDLY ■ VEGETARIAN

Any flavorful, delicate salad green, like arugula or sorrel, will do. This soup is a simplified version of Julia Child's Potage Crème de Cresson. For a stunning presentation, top the soup with freshly grated mozzarella, pickled vegetables, greens, and a drizzle of olive oil.

2 shallots, minced
2 tablespoons olive oil
Sea salt
4 cups watercress leaves and stems
3 tablespoons all-purpose flour
1½ quarts Basic Vegetable Broth (page 28), heated
1 teaspoon white wine vinegar
2 egg yolks
½ cup heavy cream

SUBSTITUTION TIP: To make this dairy-free, use coconut cream instead of heavy whipping cream. To also make it Paleo and gluten-free, use tapioca starch to thicken the soup.

Nutritional Information Calories: 228; Saturated Fat: 6g; Carbohydrates: 8g; Sodium: 621mg; Fiber: 1g; Protein: 11g

1 Heat the olive oil in a large pot over low heat. Add the shallots and a generous pinch of salt and cook for 10 minutes or until the shallots are soft and fragrant, stirring occasionally.

2 Add the watercress and pinch of salt. Cover and cook for 5 minutes.

3 Whisk in the flour and cook for 2 minutes. Pour in the vegetable broth all at once, whisk well to combine, and cook for 3 minutes or until the soup has thickened slightly. Add the white wine vinegar.

4 Purée the soup with an immersion blender. Season with salt.

5 In a large bowl, beat together the egg yolks and heavy cream. Slowly whisk in 1 cup of the soup to temper the eggs. Continue with the remaining soup until the eggs are completely integrated.

6 Return the soup to the pot and cook for 2 minutes over medium-low heat to cook the yolks. Do not simmer.

7 Serve immediately or chill, cover, and refrigerate for 2 days. This soup is also delicious when served chilled.

CELERIAC & APPLE SOUP

SERVES 4 TO 6 **PREP** 10 MINS **COOK** 20 MINS

■ PALEO ■ GLUTEN-FREE ■ VEGAN ■ BIG 8 ALLERGEN–FRIENDLY ■ FIX-AND-FORGET

I lived in England for several months, and every Friday in our small town was market day. Rain or shine (usually rain), the market served exquisite locally grown vegetables and fruit. I loved trying new produce that wasn't as common in the United States, particularly celeriac. It is a root vegetable with a flavor similar to celery, and, like celery, it pairs well with mild leeks and tart apples. Celeriac is a member of the parsley family and is in season in the winter.

1 celeriac head, peeled and diced
1 leek, white and pale green parts only, thinly sliced
2 Granny Smith apples, peeled, cored, and diced
2 celery stalks, diced
1 quart Basic Vegetable Broth (page 28)
½ cup white wine
Sea salt
1 teaspoon fresh lemon juice
1 cup fresh flat-leaf parsley leaves
½ cup olive oil
Celery leaves, for serving

1 In a large pot, mix together the celeriac, leek, apples, celery, vegetable broth, and white wine. Season with salt, bring to a gentle simmer over medium heat, and cook 20 minutes or until the vegetables are soft.

2 Add the lemon juice and purée with an immersion blender. Season with salt.

3 While the soup is cooking, combine the parsley and olive oil in a blender and purée until mostly smooth.

4 To serve, ladle the soup into individual serving bowls and garnish with celery leaves and the parsley oil.

5 Store cooled leftovers in a covered container in the refrigerator for up to 3 days.

INGREDIENT TIP: For an extra rich soup, cool the puréed soup slightly and blend in ½ cup of heavy cream.

Nutritional Information Calories: 416; Saturated Fat: 4g; Carbohydrates: 34g; Sodium: 1019mg; Fiber: 6g; Protein: 9g

FIX-AND-FORGET: To make this soup in a slow cooker, simply place all of the ingredients except the parsley and olive oil in a 4-quart slow cooker and cook on low for 6 hours or on high for 3 hours.

CREAM OF FENNEL SOUP
WITH ITALIAN SAUSAGE

SERVES 4 TO 6 **PREP** 0 MINS **COOK** 2 HOURS

■ GLUTEN-FREE

Fennel has a beautiful licorice-like aroma that mellows as it cooks. In this soup, it is present in both the creamy base as well as the spicy Italian sausage. Serve with a big loaf of crusty bread and a glass of Sangiovese.

2 tablespoons unsalted butter

2 tablespoons all-purpose flour or white rice flour

1½ quarts Roasted Vegetable Broth (page 29), heated

2 tablespoons sherry

2 fennel bulbs, cored and roughly chopped

2 links spicy Italian sausage, casings removed

½ cup heavy cream

2 egg yolks

½ cup roughly chopped fresh basil, for serving

1 In a large pot, make a roux with the butter and flour. Whisk in the heated vegetable broth and sherry. Bring to a simmer and add the chopped fennel. Cover and cook for 20 minutes or until the fennel is very soft.

2 Meanwhile, in a large pan, cook the sausage over medium-high heat until it is browned and cooked through. Set aside.

3 When the fennel is cooked through, use an immersion blender to purée the soup.

4 In a large mixing bowl, whisk together the heavy cream and egg yolks. Slowly whisk in 1 cup of the soup, then pour in the remaining soup and whisk well to combine.

5 Return the soup to the pot and cook for another 2 minutes over medium-low heat to cook the egg yolks. Do not bring to a simmer.

6 To serve, ladle the soup into individual serving bowls and top with the cooked sausage and fresh basil.

7 Serve immediately or chill, cover, and refrigerate for up to 2 days. Reheat slowly over low heat.

SUBSTITUTION TIP: For a vegetarian version of this soup, feel free to use a soy-based spicy sausage or top the soup with grated Parmesan cheese.

Nutritional Information Calories: 349; Saturated Fat: 12g; Carbohydrates: 14g; Sodium: 765mg; Fiber: 4g; Protein: 16g

PLANTAIN SOUP

SERVES 4 TO 6 **PREP** 10 MINS **COOK** 30 MINS

■ PALEO-FRIENDLY ■ GLUTEN-FREE ■ VEGAN ■ BIG 8 ALLERGEN–FRIENDLY

I discovered the delicious potential of plantains at a bright Caribbean restaurant aptly named Sunny Spot in Venice, California. They're delicious in so many applications: from fried slices to plantain mash, to this soulful, tangy soup.

4 green plantains
2 tablespoons rendered bacon fat
6 garlic cloves, minced
2 quarts Chicken Broth (page 32) or Basic Vegetable Broth (page 28)
Sea salt
Freshly ground black pepper
¼ cup fresh lime juice
1 cup sour cream, for serving
1 cup roughly chopped fresh cilantro, for serving

1 Grate the plantains using a box grater or a food processor. Set aside.

2 In a large pot, heat the bacon fat or oil over medium heat. Cook the garlic for 30 to 45 seconds or until fragrant. Pour in the broth and add the plantains. Season with salt and pepper. Cover and simmer for 25 minutes.

3 Stir in the lime juice. Purée with an immersion blender until smooth.

4 Ladle the soup into individual serving bowls and top each serving with a dollop of sour cream and a handful of cilantro.

SUBSTITUTION TIP: To make this soup vegan and Paleo, use canola oil instead of bacon fat and use diced avocados instead of sour cream.

Nutritional Information Calories: 429; Saturated Fat: 11g; Carbohydrates: 63g; Sodium: 481mg; Fiber: 4g; Protein: 7g

SOUP & COMFORT

ROASTED CARROT SOUP

SERVES 4 TO 6 **PREP** 10 MINS **COOK** 40 MINS

■ PALEO-FRIENDLY ■ GLUTEN-FREE ■ BIG 8 ALLERGEN–FRIENDLY

When I began writing this book, I asked friends and family to share their favorite soup recipes. My mom volunteered *not* to share her carrot soup. To this day, she hasn't lived down a particularly bland carrot soup that we all teased her about. But I think she was on to something—carrot soup can be absolutely exquisite! It just needs a few tweaks. Here I've paired it with brown sugar, sage, butter, and just a hint of orange zest.

2 pounds carrots, peeled and trimmed
¼ cup olive oil
Leaves from 1 sprig fresh sage
Sea salt
Freshly ground black pepper
1 quart Chicken Broth (page 32)
Zest of 1 orange
1 teaspoon apple cider vinegar
1 teaspoon packed brown sugar
4 tablespoons butter

1 Preheat the oven to 375°F.

2 In a mixing bowl, toss the carrots with the olive oil and sage leaves and then place them in a large baking dish. Season generously with salt and pepper. Roast uncovered for 30 minutes until browned and bubbling.

3 When the carrots have finished roasting, place them in a large pot with the chicken broth, orange zest, apple cider vinegar, and brown sugar. Bring the broth the a gentle simmer over medium heat. Purée with an immersion blender until smooth. For a very smooth soup, pass through a china cap.

4 Remove the pot from the heat and add the butter, 1 tablespoon at a time, puréeing after each addition.

5 Store chilled leftovers in a covered container in the refrigerator for up to 3 days.

SUBSTITUTION TIP: To make this dairy-free, omit the butter in the last step. To also make it Paleo, swap the brown sugar with coconut palm sugar or maple syrup.

Nutritional Information Calories: 326; Saturated Fat: 9g; Carbohydrates: 24g; Sodium: 569mg; Fiber: 6g; Protein: 4g

PUREED SOUPS

ROASTED EGGPLANT SOUP

SERVES 4 TO 6 **PREP** 10 MINS **COOK** 35 MINS

▪ PALEO ▪ GLUTEN-FREE ▪ VEGAN ▪ BIG 8 ALLERGEN–FRIENDLY

Eggplant is just okay in my book . . . until it is roasted. Like many vegetables, a good roast transforms it, almost magically, into something entirely different. It's creamy, savory, and absolutely scrumptious.

2 eggplants, sliced in ½-inch-thick slices
¼ cup olive oil
4 garlic cloves, minced
1 cup fresh flat-leaf parsley leaves
Zest of 1 lemon
Sea salt
Freshly ground black pepper
1 quart Basic Vegetable Broth (page 28)
1 to 2 tablespoons red wine vinegar

1 Preheat the oven to 375°F.

2 In a mixing bowl, toss the eggplant with the olive oil, garlic, parsley, and lemon zest and then spread on a sheet pan; you may need to use two pans. Season generously with salt and pepper. Roast uncovered for 30 minutes or until the eggplant pieces are wilted and sunken in the center.

3 In a large pot, mix the roasted eggplant with the chicken broth and bring to a gentle simmer. Purée with an immersion blender until smooth. For a very smooth soup, pass it through a china cap.

4 Remove the pot from the heat, stir in the vinegar, and adjust the seasonings as necessary.

5 Chill any leftover soup and store it in a covered container in the refrigerator for up to 3 days.

COOKING TIP: If you prefer a very smooth soup, peel the eggplant before roasting or remove the peels after roasting and use them as a crunchy garnish.

Nutritional Information Calories: 196; Saturated Fat: 2g; Carbohydrates: 18g; Sodium: 264mg; Fiber: 10g; Protein: 5g

LEEK & BEAN SOUP

SERVES 4 TO 6 **PREP** 10 MINS **COOK** 30 MINS

■ GLUTEN-FREE ■ VEGETARIAN ■ FIX-AND-FORGET

This puréed soup is a delicious entrée. The delicate flavor of leeks and cannellini beans is a delicious backdrop for crème fraîche and chives. It's the perfect springtime soup, especially in those climates where winter weather lingers longer than you want.

2 tablespoons unsalted butter

2 leeks, white and pale green parts only, thinly sliced

Sea salt

2 (15-ounce) cans cannellini beans, drained

1 quart chicken broth or Basic Vegetable Broth (page 28)

1 thyme sprig

1 teaspoon apple cider vinegar

Freshly ground black pepper

1 recipe Torn Baguette Croutons (page 197), for serving

4 ounces crème fraîche, for serving

4 fresh chive sprigs, snipped, for serving

FIX-AND-FORGET: To make this soup in a slow cooker, simply place all of the ingredients (except those used for serving) in a 4-quart slow cooker and cook on low for 4 hours or on high for 2 hours.

1 In a large pot, melt the butter over medium heat. Cook the leeks with a generous pinch of sea salt until softened, about 10 minutes.

2 Add the beans, broth, and thyme and bring to a simmer. Cook for 20 minutes. Remove the thyme sprig and purée the soup with an immersion blender until smooth.

3 Stir in the vinegar. Season with salt and pepper.

4 To serve, ladle the soup into serving bowls. Top each serving with croutons, a scoop of crème fraîche, and a sprinkle of fresh chives.

5 Chill, cover, and store leftovers in the refrigerator for up to 3 days. Store toppings separately accordingly to their shelf life.

SUBSTITUTION TIP: To make this soup vegan, use olive oil instead of butter and use plain coconut yogurt to top the soup. To make it gluten-free, use gluten-free bread to make the croutons or simply omit them.

Nutritional Information Calories: 337; Saturated Fat: 8g; Carbohydrates: 41g; Sodium: 642mg; Fiber: 15g; Protein: 14g

PURÉED SOUPS

ROASTED GARLIC & POTATO SOUP

SERVES 4 TO 6 **PREP** 10 MINS **COOK** 1 HOUR

■ GLUTEN-FREE ■ VEGAN ■ BIG 8 ALLERGEN–FRIENDLY ■ FIX-AND-FORGET

Whenever I read a recipe, the first thing I look at is the list of ingredients. However, I've come to discover that the preparation method for those ingredients is of far greater importance. Roasted garlic is a perfect example. Unlike its raw state, roasted garlic is subtle, sweet, rich, and absolutely decadent.

2 heads garlic
2 teaspoons olive oil
1 onion, diced
1 celery stalk, diced
2 pounds new potatoes, diced
1½ quarts Basic Vegetable Broth (page 28)
1 thyme sprig
Sea salt
Freshly ground black pepper
1 teaspoon apple cider vinegar

1 Preheat the oven to 350°F.

2 Slice the tops off both heads of garlic and place each one on a square of foil. Drizzle with the olive oil and fold the foil into loose packages. Roast for 30 minutes. Remove from the oven, open the foil packets, and allow to cool.

3 In a large pot, mix together the onion, celery, and potatoes. Cover with the broth and add the thyme sprig. Season generously with salt and pepper. Bring to a simmer, cover, and cook for 30 minutes.

4 When they are cool enough to handle, squeeze the roasted garlic cloves into the soup.

5 Remove the thyme sprig and purée the soup with an immersion blender until smooth. Stir in the vinegar. Season with salt and pepper.

6 Chill, cover, and store leftovers in the refrigerator for up to 3 days.

COOKING TIP: Get a head start on this recipe by tossing the garlic into the oven after cooking another meal. After roasting, remove the garlic from the foil squares to cool and refrigerate until ready to use.

Nutritional Information Calories: 225; Saturated Fat: 1g; Carbohydrates: 45g; Sodium: 271mg; Fiber: 7g; Protein: 7g

FIX-AND-FORGET: To make this soup in a slow cooker, simply place all of the ingredients in a 4-quart slow cooker and cook on low for 4 hours or on high for 2 hours.

ROASTED RED PEPPER & TOMATO SOUP

SERVES 4 TO 6 **PREP** 10 MINS **COOK** 20 MINS

■ PALEO ■ GLUTEN-FREE ■ VEGAN ■ BIG 8 ALLERGEN–FRIENDLY

This soup reminds me of a vegan rouille I've been making for several years. It's a delicious spread for crostini, but it's so tasty that sometimes I just want to drink it, so I turned it into a soup. Problem solved.

4 red bell peppers, cored and halved
5 tablespoons olive oil, divided
Sea salt
Freshly ground black pepper
4 garlic cloves
1 (28-ounce) can whole peeled tomatoes
1 quart Basic Vegetable Broth (page 28)
Juice of 1 lemon

COOKING TIP: Sweet bell peppers make the Dirty Dozen list year after year, so if you can afford it, purchase organic red bell peppers.

Nutritional Information Calories: 247; Saturated Fat: 3g; Carbohydrates: 19g; Sodium: 280mg; Fiber: 5g; Protein: 5g

1 Position an oven rack to the highest position and preheat the broiler.

2 Place the peppers skin-side up on a broiler pan, and flatten them with your palm. Brush with 1 tablespoon of the olive oil. Broil for about 5 minutes, until thoroughly charred. Remove the pan from the oven and transfer the peppers to a separate container. Season the peppers with salt and pepper, then cover the container and allow the peppers to steam.

3 In a large pot over medium heat, mix together the garlic cloves, tomatoes, and vegetable broth. Bring the broth to a simmer and cook for 10 minutes.

4 Remove the skins from the peppers. Roughly chop the peppers and add them to the pot. Simmer for 5 minutes. Stir in the lemon juice.

5 Purée the soup with an immersion blender until smooth. Season with salt and pepper to taste.

6 Chill, cover, and store leftovers in the refrigerator for up to 3 days.

CREAMY BROCCOLI PARMESAN SOUP

SERVES 4 TO 6 **PREP** 10 MINS **COOK** 25 MINS

■ GLUTEN-FREE ■ VEGETARIAN

This soup is just about as good as it gets. Seriously. I am so in love with the flavors of broccoli, red pepper flakes, and lemon that I can't keep them to myself. Serve with crusty bread and vegetable crudités.

2 tablespoons olive oil
1 broccoli head, cut into florets
4 garlic cloves, minced
Zest of 1 lemon
½ teaspoon red chili flakes
1 quart Chicken Broth (page 32) or Basic
  Vegetable Broth (page 28)
½ cup heavy cream
4 ounces Parmesan cheese, finely grated
Sea salt
Freshly ground black pepper

1 In a large pot, heat the olive oil over medium heat and cook the broccoli for 5 minutes.

2 Add the garlic, lemon zest, and red chili flakes and cook for 30 seconds.

3 Pour in the chicken broth and bring to a simmer. Cover and cook for 15 minutes or until the broccoli is soft.

4 Purée the soup with an immersion blender until smooth. Stir in the heavy cream and simmer for 5 minutes. Remove the pot from the heat.

5 Season with salt and pepper. Stir in the Parmesan.

6 Chill, cover, and store leftovers in the refrigerator for up to 3 days.

COOKING TIP: Always make sure to wait for a few minutes before stirring cheese into hot soup. If the temperature is too high, it can easily curdle the cheese.

Nutritional Information Calories: 264; Saturated Fat: 9g; Carbohydrates: 12g; Sodium: 464g; Fiber: 4g; Protein: 15g

PURÉED SOUPS

5

PASTA &
GRAIN-BASED SOUPS

LEMON-SCENTED ORZO & CHICKEN SOUP
WITH SPINACH

SERVES 4 TO 6 **PREP** 5 MINS **COOK** 15 MINS

■ GLUTEN-FREE ■ FIX-AND-FORGET

Orzo pasta resembles white rice but is actually made of wheat flour and shaped into tiny almond shapes. You could also use Israeli couscous, which is also made of wheat flour but is round and slightly smaller than a pencil eraser.

2 quarts Chicken Broth (page 32), plus the shredded chicken meat
2 carrots, finely diced
2 garlic cloves, minced
1 teaspoon dried Italian herb blend
Zest and juice of 1 lemon
8 ounces orzo pasta
2 cups packed spinach, cut into thin ribbons
Sea salt
Freshly ground black pepper

 FIX-AND-FORGET: To make this soup in a slow cooker, simply place all of the ingredients in a 4-quart slow cooker and cook on low for 6 hours or on high for 2 hours.

1 In a large pot over medium-high heat, bring the chicken broth to a simmer and add the shredded meat, carrots, garlic, herb blend, lemon zest, and pasta.

2 Simmer for 10 minutes until the pasta is cooked through.

3 Remove the pot from the heat and stir in the spinach and lemon juice. Season with salt and pepper.

4 Chill, cover, and store leftovers in the refrigerator for up to 3 days.

SUBSTITUTION TIP: For a gluten-free option, simply use white rice or gluten-free pasta.

Nutritional Information Calories: 445; Saturated Fat: 1g; Carbohydrates: 37g; Sodium: 754mg; Fiber: 1g; Protein: 53g

BEEF BARLEY SOUP

SERVES 4 TO 6 **PREP** 10 MINS **COOK** 50 MINS

■ BIG 8 ALLERGEN–FRIENDLY

Growing up, my mom always kept a large stock of whole grains, such as barley and wheat berries. With a little bit of meat and some vegetables, they could easily expand to fill a pot and hungry tummies. Ask me later about the time I tried to wash several cups of stale wheat berries down the kitchen sink—suffice it to say, they expand.

1 tablespoon olive oil
1 pound beef chuck, cut into
   ½-inch pieces
Sea salt
Freshly ground black pepper
1 onion, diced
2 carrots, diced
2 celery stalks, diced
6 garlic cloves, smashed
2 quarts Beef Stock (page 35)
2 tablespoons tomato paste
1½ cups pearl barley
Bouquet garni of fresh herbs, such as
   rosemary, thyme, and parsley

1   In a large pot, heat the olive oil over medium-high heat. Pat the beef dry with paper towels and season with salt and pepper. Brown on all sides, about 10 minutes total.

2   Add the onion, carrots, celery, and garlic to the pan and cook for 5 minutes.

3   Pour in the beef broth and tomato paste and bring to a simmer.

4   Add the pearl barley and bouquet garni. Season the broth with salt and pepper, cover the pot, and cook for 40 minutes until the barley is soft.

5   Remove the herbs and discard. Taste the soup and adjust the seasonings as needed.

6   Chill, cover, and store leftovers in the refrigerator for up to 4 days.

SUBSTITUTION TIP: Barley contains the protein gluten. To make this gluten-free, use brown rice, quinoa, or another gluten-free whole grain.

Nutritional Information Calories: 573; Saturated Fat: 3g; Carbohydrates: 69g; Sodium: 765mg; Fiber: 14g; Protein: 45g

SWEDISH MEATBALL SOUP
WITH CABBAGE & PASTA

SERVES 4 TO 6 **PREP** 15 MINS **COOK** 35 MINS

■ GLUTEN-FREE

In the darkest days of winter, the warm spices in the meatballs and the sturdy beef broth offer warmth and comfort. To save time, you can use pre-made Swedish meatballs (without gravy) if you wish.

1 slice white bread, crusts removed
¼ cup milk
½ pound ground beef
½ pound ground pork
¼ cup minced onion
¼ teaspoon ground allspice
¼ teaspoon freshly ground nutmeg
Sea salt
Freshly ground black pepper
1 egg, lightly beaten
2 quarts Beef Stock (page 35)
8 ounces elbow macaroni noodles
4 cups roughly chopped cabbage leaves

SUBSTITUTION TIP: To make this gluten-free, use gluten-free bread and gluten-free pasta.

Nutritional Information Calories: 485; Saturated Fat: 3g; Carbohydrates: 50g; Sodium: 876mg; Fiber: 4g; Protein: 50g

1 Preheat the oven to 375°F. Line a baking sheet with parchment paper.

2 In a medium bowl, soak the bread in the milk. Set aside.

3 In a mixing bowl, mix together the beef, pork, onion, allspice, and nutmeg. Wring the excess milk from the bread and add the bread to the meat mixture. Season with salt and pepper and mix well with your hands.

4 Form the meat mixture into about 24 medium-size meatballs and place them on the prepared baking sheet. Bake for 30 minutes until browned.

5 During the last 10 minutes of baking time, bring the beef stock to a simmer in a large pot and cook the macaroni noodles for 5 minutes.

6 Add the cabbage and meatballs to the stock and cook for 5 minutes. Season with salt and pepper.

7 Serve immediately or chill, cover, and store leftovers in the refrigerator for up to 4 days.

WILD RICE & TURKEY SOUP

SERVES 4 TO 6 **PREP** 10 MINS **COOK** 55 MINS

■ GLUTEN-FREE ■ BIG 8 ALLERGEN—FRIENDLY

My mom always made this simple soup the day after Thanksgiving to use up turkey leftovers. I'm partial to dark meat, but you can use whatever you have. It's an easy recipe designed to give you a break in the kitchen. Feel free to thicken the soup with a few scoops of mashed potatoes as well, if you have extra.

2 tablespoons olive oil
1 onion, diced
4 celery stalks, diced
4 carrots, diced
2 quarts Chicken Broth (page 32)
Sea salt
Freshly ground black pepper
1 bay leaf
1 cup wild rice
4 cups shredded cooked turkey

1 In a large pot, heat the olive oil over medium heat and cook the onion, celery, and carrots for 10 minutes, until they have softened.

2 Pour in the chicken broth, season generously with salt and pepper, and add the bay leaf.

3 Bring to a simmer and stir in the wild rice and turkey.

4 Cover and cook for 45 minutes, or until the rice is al dente.

5 Chill, cover, and store leftovers in the refrigerator for up to 3 days.

SUBSTITUTION TIP: If you don't have turkey, feel free to use the cooked chicken from the Chicken Broth (page 32).

Nutritional Information Calories: 482; Saturated Fat: 3g; Carbohydrates: 39g; Sodium: 501mg; Fiber: 5g; Protein: 48g

RAINY DAY CHICKEN NOODLE SOUP

SERVES 4 TO 6 **PREP** 10 MINS **COOK** 20 MINS

■ PALEO ■ GLUTEN-FREE ■ BIG 8 ALLERGEN—FRIENDLY

Just a friendly warning: Once you start making your chicken noodle soup from scratch, you'll never be able to go back to store-bought soup again! I suggest using the Roasted Chicken Stock (page 31), but the Chicken Broth (page 32) also works well. I like to use loads of garlic because it is part of what makes chicken soup so good for you, especially when cold and flu season rolls around.

2 tablespoons olive oil
2 pounds boneless, skinless chicken
  thighs, cut into 2-inch pieces
Sea salt
Freshly ground black pepper
4 carrots, thinly sliced
4 celery stalks, thinly sliced
6 to 8 garlic cloves, thinly sliced
2 quarts Roasted Chicken Stock (page 31)
1 tablespoon chopped fresh thyme
8 ounces wide egg noodles
1 teaspoon apple cider vinegar

1 In a large pot, heat the olive oil over medium-high heat. Season the chicken with salt and pepper and place it in the pan. Allow the meat to brown for 2 to 3 minutes, stirring to brown on all sides.

2 Add the carrots, celery, and garlic and cook for 5 minutes, stirring constantly, until the vegetables have begun to soften. Pour in the chicken stock and add the thyme. Bring the stock to a simmer, cook for 5 minutes, then add the egg noodles. Simmer for 5 minutes, until the noodles are tender.

3 Stir in the vinegar and adjust the seasonings to taste.

4 Chill, cover, and store any leftovers in the refrigerator for up to 3 days.

SUBSTITUTION TIP: To make this soup gluten-free, replace the egg noodles with gluten-free noodles. I find that corn-based noodles have the best texture. To make this soup Paleo, simply omit the noodles entirely.

Nutritional Information Calories: 763; Saturated Fat: 8g; Carbohydrates: 49g; Sodium: 602mg; Fiber: 4g; Protein: 62g

MATZO BALL SOUP

SERVES 4 TO 6 **PREP** 10 MINS **COOK** 25 MINS

■ GLUTEN-FREE ■ VEGETARIAN

One of the many restaurants I worked at while in college was a New York–style deli with Reubens, matzo ball soup, bagels, and specialty cakes by the slice. I never learned to love the corned beef sandwiches, but the matzo ball soup became my lunch break favorite—okay, and sometimes just a piece of cake. Each of the matzo balls was so large that we could barely fit it into the ladle, and each serving included one of the dumplings.

3 large eggs, whisked
¾ cup matzo meal
¼ cup schmaltz, melted
3 tablespoons soda water
1 teaspoon kosher salt
1 recipe Chicken Broth (page 32) plus the reserved chicken meat, shredded
2 carrots, thinly sliced
2 tablespoons roughly chopped fresh dill
Sea salt
Freshly ground black pepper

1 In a small bowl, mix together the eggs, matzo meal, schmaltz, soda water, and kosher salt. Cover the bowl and let the mixture rest in the refrigerator for 1 hour or up to 12 hours if you prefer to make it ahead of time.

2 In a large pot over medium heat, bring the chicken broth to a gentle simmer.

3 Form the matzo dough into 3-inch balls and carefully place them into the broth. Cover the pot and cook for 20 to 25 minutes until cooked through. Be careful not to let the broth come to a boil, which could break up the matzo balls.

4 During the last 5 minutes of cooking, add the carrots, dill, and shredded chicken to the broth. Season with salt and pepper.

5 Cool any leftover soup, cover, and store in the refrigerator for up to 2 days.

SUBSTITUTION TIP: If you need a wheat- and gluten-free soup, you can purchase gluten-free matzo meal online. To make it vegetarian, simply use Basic Vegetable Broth (page 28) and butter in place of the schmaltz.

Nutritional Information Calories: 253; Saturated Fat: 8g; Carbohydrates: 21g; Sodium: 987mg; Fiber: 2g; Protein: 8g

SOUP & COMFORT

MINESTRONE

SERVES 4 TO 6 **PREP** 10 MINS **COOK** 30 MINS

▪ GLUTEN-FREE ▪ VEGAN ▪ BIG 8 ALLERGEN–FRIENDLY

Whenever I think of the story *Stone Soup*, I always think of minestrone. Perhaps it is because many of the soups my mom made resembled it—a few vegetables, beans, and pasta. If you have a good broth, you can add whatever fresh vegetables and herbs you have on hand.

2 tablespoons olive oil
1 onion, diced
3 garlic cloves, minced
2 celery stalks, diced
2 carrots, diced
2 cups green beans , trimmed and cut into 2-inch pieces
1 tablespoon dried Italian herb blend
1 (28-ounce) can whole peeled tomatoes, hand crushed
1½ quarts Basic Vegetable Broth (page 28) or Chicken Broth (page 32)
Sea salt
Freshly ground black pepper
8 ounces elbow macaroni noodles
1 (15-ounce) can kidney beans, rinsed and drained

1 Heat the olive oil in a large pot over medium-high heat and cook the onion, garlic, celery, and carrots for 5 minutes. Add the green beans, herb blend, and tomatoes, and cook for another 2 to 3 minutes.

2 Pour in the vegetable broth, season with salt and pepper, bring the mixture to a simmer, and cook for 10 more minutes or until the vegetables are tender.

3 Add the pasta and kidney beans, cover the pot, and cook for 10 minutes or until the pasta is tender. Adjust the seasonings as needed.

4 Serve immediately or chill, cover, and store the soup in the refrigerator for up to 4 days.

COOKING TIP: To make this gluten- and wheat-free, use gluten-free noodles.

Nutritional Information Calories: 445; Saturated Fat: 1g; Carbohydrates: 76g; Sodium: 770mg; Fiber: 13g; Protein: 16g

SOUTHWESTERN QUINOA SOUP
WITH CORN & RED PEPPER

SERVES 4 TO 6 **PREP** 10 MINS **COOK** 30 MINS

■ GLUTEN-FREE ■ VEGAN ■ BIG 8 ALLERGEN–FRIENDLY ■ FIX-AND-FORGET

When quinoa first gained popularity, I'll admit I was nervous to cook it because I didn't know how to pronounce it. In case you're still wondering, it's *keen-wah*. This nutty little seed, sometimes called a pseudo-grain, is packed with protein and fiber and makes a filling meal.

2 tablespoons olive oil

1 onion, minced

2 garlic cloves, minced

2 medium potatoes, peeled and diced

2 red bell peppers, diced

2 cups diced green beans

1 teaspoon ground cumin

1 chipotle in adobo sauce, minced, plus 1 tablespoon adobo sauce

1 (15-ounce) can diced fire-roasted tomatoes, with juices

2 quarts Basic Vegetable Broth (page 28)

2 cups quinoa

Sea salt

Freshly ground black pepper

1 tablespoon fresh lime juice

1 In a large pot, heat the olive oil over medium heat and cook the onion and garlic for 5 minutes. Add the potatoes, peppers, and green beans and cook for 2 minutes.

2 Stir in the cumin and chipotle with adobo sauce. Pour in the tomatoes, broth, and quinoa. Season generously with salt and pepper. Cover and cook for 25 minutes.

3 Stir in the lime juice and adjust the seasonings as necessary.

4 Chill, cover, and store leftovers in the refrigerator for up to 3 days.

INGREDIENT TIP: For additional protein, add grilled sliced steak or cooked chicken tenderloins after the onions have cooked.

Nutritional Information Calories: 626; Saturated Fat: 2g; Carbohydrates: 112g; Sodium: 683mg; Fiber: 22g; Protein: 21g

FIX-AND-FORGET: To make this soup in a slow cooker, simply place all of the ingredients in a 4-quart slow cooker and cook on low for 3 hours or on high for 1 hour and 30 minutes.

ITALIAN WEDDING SOUP

SERVES 4 TO 6 **PREP** 15 MINS **COOK** 45 MINS

■ GLUTEN-FREE

I read an essay on NPR recently about an Indian man who moved to the American Midwest, where he found delicious Indian food but, ironically, longed for the versions of American dishes he had enjoyed in India. Often when a foreign dish is adopted by a new culture, it takes on a completely original flavor not present in the original dish. Italian wedding soup is a classic example. Wedding soup, as we know it, is largely an American creation, a mistranslation of the Italian *minestra maritata* referring to the delicious marriage of meat and vegetables. So, while you won't find this version on the menu in Italy, it is filling and delicious, and it's just a lovely sounding name.

½ cup bread crumbs
¼ cup milk
½ pound ground veal
¾ pound ground pork
1 teaspoon minced garlic
1 teaspoon dried oregano
1 egg, lightly beaten
2 ounces Parmesan cheese, finely grated
Sea salt
Freshly ground black pepper
2 tablespoons olive oil
1 onion, diced
2 carrots, diced
2 celery stalks, diced
½ cup dry white wine
2 quarts Roasted Chicken Stock (page 31)
4 ounces orzo pasta
1 bunch Lacinato kale, ribs removed,
*   leaves thinly sliced*
4 cups spinach leaves, thinly sliced
1 cup fresh basil leaves, roughly chopped

1 Preheat the oven to 375°F. Line a baking sheet with parchment paper.

2 In a small bowl, soak the bread crumbs in the milk; set aside.

3 In a large mixing bowl, mix together the veal, pork, garlic, oregano, egg, and Parmesan. Squeeze the excess milk out of the bread crumbs and add the bread crumbs to the meat mixture. Season with salt and pepper. Mix with your hands.

4 Form the meat mixture into about 36 teaspoon-size meatballs and place them on the prepared baking sheet. Bake for 25 minutes, until browned.

5 While the meatballs bake, heat the olive oil in a large pot over medium heat and add the onion, carrots, celery, and a generous pinch of salt. Cook for 10 minutes, stirring frequently, until the vegetables have softened.

6 Add the white wine and sauté for 2 to 3 minutes to cook off some of the alcohol. Pour in the chicken stock and bring to a simmer.

7 Add the pasta and cook for 5 minutes, until soft.

8 Add the kale and the meatballs and cook for 2 minutes. Remove the pot from the heat and stir in the spinach and basil. Season with salt and pepper.

9 Serve immediately or chill, cover, and store leftovers in the refrigerator for up to 4 days.

SUBSTITUTION TIP: To make this soup free of wheat and gluten, use gluten-free bread crumbs and gluten-free pasta.

Nutritional Information Calories: 595; Saturated Fat: 7g; Carbohydrates: 45g; Sodium: 798mg; Fiber: 5g; Protein: 53g

TORTELLINI TOMATO BASIL SOUP

SERVES 4 TO 6 **PREP** 10 MINS **COOK** 20 MINS

■ VEGETARIAN

This soup has similar flavors to Italian Wedding Soup (page 100) but takes a fraction of the time to prepare. It also uses ingredients you probably already have in your pantry.

2 tablespoons olive oil

1 onion, diced

1 carrot, finely diced

1 celery stalk, finely diced

4 garlic cloves, minced

1 teaspoon dried oregano

1 (28-ounce) can whole peeled tomatoes, hand crushed

1 quart Chicken Broth (page 32) or Basic Vegetable Broth (page 28)

Sea salt

Freshly ground black pepper

16 ounces fresh sausage-filled tortellini

1 cup fresh basil leaves, roughly chopped

4 ounces Parmesan cheese, finely grated, for serving

1 In a large pot, heat the olive oil over medium heat. Cook the onion, carrot, celery, and garlic for 5 minutes. Add the oregano, tomatoes, and broth; bring to a simmer. Season with salt and pepper.

2 Add the tortellini and cook for 5 to 7 minutes, or according to the directions on the package.

3 Remove the pot from the heat and stir in the fresh basil leaves.

4 To serve, ladle the soup into individual serving bowls and garnish with Parmesan cheese.

5 Chill, cover, and store leftovers in the refrigerator for up to 3 days.

SUBSTITUTION TIP: For a vegetarian version of the soup, use cheese-filled tortellini.

Nutritional Information Calories: 409; Saturated Fat: 6g; Carbohydrates: 48g; Sodium: 954mg; Fiber: 5g; Protein: 21g

BLACK RICE WITH CHICKEN & MANGO

SERVES 4 TO 6 **PREP** 5 MINS **COOK** 30 MINS

▪ GLUTEN-FREE ▪ BIG 8 ALLERGEN–FRIENDLY ▪ FIX-AND-FORGET

The flavor of black rice is similar to that of wild rice but with a uniform texture and color. I love the contrasting color of the bright yellow mango and green scallions. The Southeast Asian flavors of ginger, garlic, chili flakes, and fish sauce are the perfect balance of salty, sour, sweet, and spicy.

2 quarts Chicken Broth (page 32) with shredded chicken meat
1 teaspoon minced fresh ginger
1 teaspoon minced garlic
¼ teaspoon red chili flakes
1 tablespoon fish sauce
1 cup black rice
2 cups sugar snap peas, cut into ½-inch pieces
1 mango, peeled and diced
2 tablespoons fresh lime juice
2 scallions, thinly sliced, for serving

1 In a large pot over medium heat, bring the chicken broth to a simmer.

2 Add the ginger, garlic, red chili flakes, and fish sauce. Cook for 1 minute.

3 Stir in the black rice, cover the pot, and cook for 30 minutes or until the rice is tender.

4 Remove the lid from the pot and stir in the chicken, snap peas, and mango. Cook for 2 minutes to meld the flavors.

5 Stir in the lime juice and garnish with the scallions.

SUBSTITUTION TIP: For an allergen-free soup, omit the fish sauce and use a pinch of sea salt.

Nutritional Information Calories: 297; Saturated Fat: 0g; Carbohydrates: 58g; Sodium: 494mg; Fiber: 7g; Protein: 14g

FIX-AND-FORGET: To make this soup in a slow cooker, simply add all of the ingredients except mango to a 4-quart slow cooker and cook on low for 6 hours or on high for 2 hours and 30 minutes. For an optional extra step, you can add the mango at the end, after the soup is cooked.

PHO

SERVES 4 TO 6 **PREP** 15 MINS **COOK** 1 HOUR

■ GLUTEN-FREE ■ BIG 8 ALLERGEN–FRIENDLY

In college I worked as a writer for *The Asian Reporter*, a community newspaper in Portland. That's when I fell in love with Asian food and hospitality. One of the stories I covered sent me to a Vietnamese restaurant in Southeast Portland where I tasted pho for the first time. (The hipster in me wants you to know this was before pho was popular.) The flavors were surprising and addicting, each bite with a slightly different texture and flavor than the last.

1 onion, sliced into thick rings
1 tablespoon canola oil
1-inch knob peeled fresh ginger
2 cinnamon sticks
8 star anise
1 lemongrass shoot, halved
2 quarts Beef Stock (page 35)
1 tablespoon fish sauce
8 ounces wide rice noodles
1 pound flank steak, very thinly sliced
1 cup fresh cilantro, for serving
½ cup fresh basil leaves, for serving
½ cup fresh mint leaves, for serving
2 scallions, thinly sliced on a bias, for serving
1 cup bean sprouts, for serving
2 limes, cut into wedges, for serving

1 Set an oven rack in the highest position and preheat the broiler.

2 Spread the onion slices on a broiler pan and brush them with the oil. Transfer the pan to the top rack of the oven and broil until the onions are charred, about 5 minutes.

3 In a large pot over medium heat, mix the onion with the ginger, cinnamon, star anise, lemongrass, and beef stock. Bring the liquid to a simmer, cover the pot, and cook for 1 hour to infuse the stock with flavor.

4 Strain the soup through a fine-mesh sieve into a clean pot, discarding the solids, and return it to the heat. Stir in the fish sauce and bring the liquid back to a simmer.

5 Meanwhile, prepare the rice noodles by soaking them in cold water for 30 minutes, or according to the package directions. Divide the noodles among individual serving bowls.

6 Top the noodles with the raw beef slices and immediately pour the hot beef broth over them. Allow each person to add cilantro, basil, mint, scallions, and bean sprouts as desired. Serve with lime wedges.

7 Chill and store the leftover soup components separately in a covered container in the refrigerator for up to 3 days.

SUBSTITUTION TIP: For allergen-free soup, omit the fish sauce. To get razor-thin slices of the steak, place it in the freezer for 20 minutes to firm the flesh up slightly and use a very sharp chef's knife to cut it.

Nutritional Information Calories: 529; Saturated Fat: 4g; Carbohydrates: 57g; Sodium: 1302mg; Fiber: 5g; Protein: 46g

CHICKEN FAUX PHO

SERVES 4 TO 6 **PREP** 10 MINS **COOK** 1 HOUR

■ GLUTEN-FREE ■ BIG 8 ALLERGEN–FRIENDLY

Endless wordplay can be had with the word *pho*. The restaurant 9021PHO proves my point. The thing is, the pronunciation of the classic Vietnamese dish is actually "fuh." So here's my not-so-authentic take on the noodle soup using chicken broth and shredded chicken.

2 quarts Chicken Broth (page 32), plus chicken meat, shredded
2 cinnamon sticks
8 star anise
1 lemongrass shoot
2 tablespoons fish sauce
¼ cup soy sauce
8 ounces rice noodles
1 cup fresh cilantro leaves, for serving
½ cup fresh basil leaves, for serving
¼ cup fresh mint leaves, for serving
2 scallions, thinly sliced on a bias
Bean sprouts
2 limes, cut into wedges, for serving

1 In a large pot over medium heat, combine the chicken broth, cinnamon, star anise, and lemongrass. Bring the liquid to a simmer and cook for 1 hour.

2 Strain the broth through a fine-mesh sieve into a clean pot and discard the solids.

3 Stir in the fish sauce and soy sauce.

4 Meanwhile, prepare the rice noodles by soaking them in cold water for 30 minutes, or according to the package directions. Divide the noodles among individual serving bowls and top with the shredded chicken.

5 Pour the chicken broth over each bowl and allow each person to add cilantro, basil, mint, scallions, and bean sprouts as desired. Serve with lime wedges.

6 Chill and store the leftover soup components separately in covered containers in the refrigerator for up to 3 days.

SUBSTITUTION TIP: For allergen-free soup, omit the fish sauce. To save time, add the cinnamon, star anise, and lemongrass to the Chicken Broth (page 32) when you make it.

Nutritional Information Calories: 376; Saturated Fat: 3g; Carbohydrates: 19g; Sodium: 1869mg; Fiber: 1g; Protein: 47g

QUICK & EASY RAMEN

SERVES 4 TO 6 **PREP** 5 MINS **COOK** 5 MINS

■ VEGAN

I could have lived on ramen as a child. What I didn't realize then was how nutritionally deficient packaged ramen noodles were. Worse than the nutrients it didn't contain was what it did: you know, just a little monosodium glutamate (MSG). Fortunately, you can find naturally occurring glutamic acid in mushrooms and celery, both of which are present in the Roasted Vegetable Broth (page 29).

2 quarts Roasted Vegetable Broth
(page 29) or Chicken Broth (page 32)
1 teaspoon minced garlic
2 cups finely diced carrots
2 cups frozen peas, defrosted
1 tablespoon soy sauce
1 tablespoon fresh lime juice
16 ounces refrigerated yakisoba noodles
2 scallions, thinly sliced
Sea salt
Freshly ground black pepper

1 In a large pot, bring the broth to a simmer over medium heat. Add the garlic, carrots, and peas. Cook for 2 minutes.

2 Stir in the soy sauce and lime juice and cook for 1 minute.

3 Add the noodles and cook according to the package directions.

4 Stir in the scallions. Season with salt and pepper.

5 Chill, cover, and store leftover broth in the refrigerator for up to 3 days. Heat before serving and add the noodles.

INGREDIENT TIP: Want a little more substance in this soup? Use Chicken Broth (page 32) and add the shredded chicken meat.

Nutritional Information Calories: 327; Saturated Fat: 0g; Carbohydrates: 59g; Sodium: 987mg; Fiber: 7g; Protein: 14g

POSOLE

SERVES 4 TO 6 **PREP** 10 MINS **COOK** 3 HOURS, 30 MINS

■ GLUTEN-FREE ■ BIG 8 ALLERGEN–FRIENDLY

I first enjoyed this soup at a Phoenix restaurant that featured Mexico City cuisine. Even though it was well over 100 degrees outside, somehow the light and spicy soup hit the spot. It is easy to prepare and fun to share with friends.

1 (2-pound) boneless pork shoulder

1 tablespoon plus ½ teaspoon smoked paprika, divided

1 tablespoon plus 1 teaspoon ground cumin, divided

Sea salt

Freshly ground black pepper

2 tablespoons canola oil

2 red onions, halved and thinly sliced, divided

1 cup water

2 tablespoons olive oil

4 garlic cloves, minced

4 cups diced fresh tomatoes

2 quarts Basic Vegetable Broth (page 28)

1 teaspoon dried oregano

2 (8-ounce) cans white hominy, drained

1 cup fresh cilantro leaves, for serving

1 bunch radishes, thinly sliced, for serving

4 limes, halved, for serving

8 to 12 corn tortillas, for serving

1 Preheat the oven to 325°F.

2 Coat the pork with 1 tablespoon each of the paprika and cumin. Season generously with salt and pepper.

3 Heat the canola oil in a Dutch oven over high heat. Brown the pork on all sides.

4 Add half of the onions to the pot and pour in 1 cup of water. Place the pot in the oven and braise for 2 to 3 hours, until the pork is tender and easy to shred with a fork.

5 In a separate large pot, heat the olive oil over medium heat. Cook the remaining onion, garlic, and tomatoes for 10 minutes, stirring frequently, until the vegetables are soft.

6 Add the broth, oregano, remaining 1 teaspoon cumin, and remaining ½ teaspoon paprika. Bring the liquid to a simmer and cook for 5 minutes. Add the hominy and cook for 5 more minutes.

7 When the pork has finished cooking, shred it with a fork and stir it into the soup.

8 Ladle the soup into individual serving bowls and allow each person to garnish with cilantro, radishes, limes, and corn tortillas.

9 Chill, cover, and store the leftover soup and toppings separately in the refrigerator for up to 3 days.

COOKING TIP: You can also purchase pre-cooked shredded pork if you prefer not to heat up your kitchen for this recipe!

Nutritional Information Calories: 718; Saturated Fat: 5g; Carbohydrates: 58g; Sodium: 468mg; Fiber: 12g; Protein: 67g

6

SEAFOOD SOUPS
& CHOWDERS

BOUILLABAISSE

SERVES 4 TO 6 **PREP** 10 MINS **COOK** 30 MINS

■ PALEO ■ GLUTEN-FREE

Like many classic French soups and stews, Bouillabaisse is an economical, resourceful use of whatever is available. For fishermen living along the Mediterranean coast, it is the day's catch, which could include a tremendous variety of small fish and shellfish. Wherever you live, use sustainably caught fresh fish and shellfish in season or frozen fish.

1 tablespoon olive oil

1 leek, white and pale green parts only, halved lengthwise and thinly sliced

1 onion, diced

1 fennel bulb, cored and thinly sliced

4 garlic cloves, thinly sliced

1 teaspoon fennel seeds, coarsely ground

¼ teaspoon red chili flakes

3 plum tomatoes, cored and diced

½ cup dry white wine or vermouth

2 quarts Seafood Stock (page 36)

1 (2-inch) piece orange peel

Pinch saffron

Sea salt

3 to 4 pounds fresh fish and shellfish, such as cod, flounder, scallops, prawns, halibut, clams, and mussels, cleaned and cut (if needed) into 2-inch pieces

½ cup roughly chopped fresh flat-leaf parsley, for serving

1 Heat the oil in a large pot over medium heat. Add the leek, onion, fennel bulb, garlic, fennel seeds, and chili flakes and cook for 5 minutes until slightly softened.

2 Add the tomatoes and cook for 1 minute.

3 Pour in the wine and cook for 2 minutes. Add the seafood stock, orange peel, and saffron. Season with salt. Simmer gently for 10 minutes.

4 If you're using clams or mussels, place them in the pot and cook for 5 to 7 minutes, until the shells open. Discard any that have not opened after 10 minutes. Remove the cooked shellfish to a heat-proof dish.

5 If you're using large prawns, add them to the pan, cover, and cook for 5 minutes (smaller ones can be added with the fish). Then, add the remaining seafood. Cover and cook for 5 to 7 minutes or until the fish is opaque.

6 Return the shellfish to the soup and stir in the fresh parsley. Serve immediately.

7 To store leftovers, cool, cover, and refrigerate for up to 2 days.

PAIRING TIP: The classic accompaniment to Bouillabaisse is a sauce called rouille. To make it, purée 2 garlic cloves, 1 peeled roasted red pepper, 1 egg yolk, 1 teaspoon red wine vinegar, and a pinch of sea salt in a blender. With the motor running, slowly drizzle in ½ cup of olive oil. Serve drizzled over the soup or as a spread on crusty bread.

Nutritional Information Calories: 677; Saturated Fat: 6g; Carbohydrates: 19g; Sodium: 854mg; Fiber: 4g; Protein: 71g

CIOPPINO SEAFOOD STEW

SERVES 4 TO 6 **PREP** 15 MINS **COOK** 2 HOURS

■ PALEO ■ GLUTEN-FREE

If Bouillabaisse had a wildly eccentric American cousin, it would be Cioppino. This flavorful soup originated in San Francisco where the day's catch determines its exact ingredients. In a city that sees so many days of heavy fog, Cioppino's piquant warmth is the perfect antidote. I especially enjoy it after a long day of surfing in the fall when water temperatures dip below 60 degrees.

¼ cup olive oil

6 garlic cloves, minced

1 onion, diced

1 fennel bulb, cored and diced

1 bay leaf

1 teaspoon fennel seeds, coarsely ground

½ teaspoon red chili flakes

½ teaspoon dried oregano or
   1 teaspoon chopped fresh oregano

Sea salt

1 red bell pepper, cored and diced

1½ cups full-bodied red wine

2 tablespoons tomato paste

1 (28-ounce) can whole peeled tomatoes,
   hand crushed

2 cups Seafood Stock (page 36)

Freshly ground black pepper

3 to 4 pounds fresh fish and shellfish,
   such as halibut, crab legs, scallops,
   prawns, clams, and mussels, cleaned
   and cut (if needed) into 2-inch pieces

¼ cup roughly chopped fresh flat-
   leaf parsley

1. In a large pot, mix together the olive oil, garlic, onion, fennel bulb, bay leaf, fennel seeds, red chili flakes, and oregano and season with a generous pinch of salt. Cook for 5 minutes over medium heat until the onion is slightly softened.

2. Add the bell pepper and cook for another 1 to 2 minutes.

3. Pour in the red wine and cook for 5 minutes, allowing some of the alcohol to evaporate.

4. Stir in the tomato paste, tomatoes, and seafood stock. Cover and cook for 20 minutes. Season with salt and pepper.

5. If you're using clams, mussels, or crab, place them in the pot and cook for 5 to 7 minutes, until the shells open. Discard any that have not opened after 10 minutes. Remove the cooked shellfish to a heat-proof dish.

6. If you're using large prawns, add them to the pan, cover, and cook for 5 minutes (smaller ones can be added with the fish). Then, add the remaining seafood. Cover and cook for 5 to 7 minutes, or until the fish is opaque.

7. Return the shellfish to the soup and stir in the fresh parsley. Serve immediately.

8. To store leftovers, cool, cover, and refrigerate for up to 2 days.

COOKING TIP: Get a head start on this recipe by making the soup without the seafood a day ahead of time. Simply bring it to a simmer just before serving and add the fish and shellfish as described above.

Nutritional Information Calories: 553; Saturated Fat: 3g; Carbohydrates: 22g; Sodium: 632g; Fiber: 5g; Protein: 67g

BOURRIDE

SERVES 4 TO 6 **PREP** 15 MINS **COOK** 45 MINS

■ PALEO-FRIENDLY ■ GLUTEN-FREE

The first time I made Bourride, I expected something akin to Bouillabaisse, given that the ingredients are so similar. While the flavors are nearly identical, the texture and presentation of Bourride are truly unique. The broth is perfectly smooth and thickened with a simple garlic aioli, with the seafood set artfully in the center of each bowl.

FOR THE AIOLI

1 egg yolk
2 teaspoons fresh lemon juice
1 garlic clove, minced
Sea salt
¼ cup olive oil
¾ cup canola oil

FOR THE BROTH

1 tablespoon olive oil
2 leeks, white and pale green parts only, halved lengthwise and thinly sliced
2 onions, diced
4 garlic cloves, thinly sliced
1 teaspoon fennel seeds, coarsely ground
¼ teaspoon red chili flakes
3 plum tomatoes, cored and diced
Sea salt
1 cup dry white wine
1 quart Seafood Stock (page 36)
Pinch saffron
3 to 4 pounds fresh fish and shellfish, such as scallops, prawns, monkfish, sea bass, and halibut cleaned and cut (if needed) into 2-inch pieces
½ cup roughly chopped fresh flat-leaf parsley, for serving

TO MAKE THE AIOLI

1 In a medium bowl, whisk together the egg yolk, lemon juice, garlic, and a pinch of sea salt.

2 Slowly drizzle in the olive and canola oils, whisking constantly until emulsified.

3 Let the aioli rest in the refrigerator while you prepare the soup.

TO MAKE THE BROTH

1 In a large pot, mix together the olive oil, leeks, onions, garlic, fennel seeds, red chili flakes, and tomatoes and season with salt. Cook over medium heat for 15 minutes. Add the wine and cook for 5 minutes before adding the seafood stock. Cook for another 15 minutes.

2 Strain the broth through a fine-mesh sieve into a large bowl, discarding the solids. Wipe out the pot and return the broth to it. Bring the broth to a gentle simmer and add the saffron and seafood. Cover and cook until the clams have opened (if using) and the fish is opaque, 5 to 7 minutes. Remove the seafood from the pot and divide it among individual serving bowls.

3 Remove about ½ cup of the broth from the pot and whisk it into the aioli. Then pour the aioli into the hot broth and cook over gentle heat for 3 minutes, until slightly thickened.

4 Use a ladle to pour the soup around the seafood in each bowl. Garnish with fresh parsley.

5 Given that the soup is thickened with egg yolk, it is very difficult to reheat and is therefore best enjoyed immediately.

SUBSTITUTION TIP: If you want to make this Paleo, use only olive oil or a mix of olive and macadamia oils in the aioli. However, be aware that extra-virgin olive oil tends to have an overpowering flavor.

Nutritional Information Calories: 923; Saturated Fat: 7g; Carbohydrates: 20g; Sodium: 431g; Fiber: 4g; Protein: 67g

SHRIMP BISQUE

SERVES 4 TO 6 **PREP** 10 MINS **COOK** 20 MINS

■ GLUTEN-FREE

This spicy and savory soup makes a delicious entrée. Simply serve with crusty bread and a glass of Riesling. If you're serving this to children, start with ¼ teaspoon cayenne pepper and increase to suit their tastes.

4 tablespoons unsalted butter
¼ cup all-purpose flour or white rice flour
1½ quarts Seafood Stock (page 36)
Zest of 1 orange
½ teaspoon cayenne pepper
2 tablespoons tomato paste
1 cup heavy cream
1½ pounds large shrimp, peeled
Sea salt
Freshly ground black pepper

1 In a large pot, cook the butter and flour over medium heat for 2 minutes, whisking constantly, until bubbling and thick.

2 Pour in the seafood stock, whisking to distribute the roux. Add the orange zest, cayenne, and tomato paste. Simmer for 5 minutes to thicken.

3 Add the heavy cream and simmer for 5 more minutes, then stir in the shrimp and simmer until the shrimp are opaque and cooked through. Season with salt and pepper.

4 Chill, cover, and store any leftovers in the refrigerator for up to 2 days.

SUBSTITUTION TIP: To make this gluten-free, use gluten-free flour such as white rice flour or sorghum flour for thickening.

Nutritional Information Calories: 397; Saturated Fat: 15g; Carbohydrates: 12g; Sodium: 554mg; Fiber: 1g; Protein: 37g

CRAB BISQUE

SERVES 4 TO 6 **PREP** 10 MINS **COOK** 15 MINS

■ GLUTEN-FREE

I absolutely love the flavors of mint and crab together. It is a classic flavor combination and is exquisite in this creamy soup. You can leave out the Parmesan if you wish, but it gives the soup an added layer of flavor and texture. Make sure to float several Torn Baguette Croutons (page 197) in the soup just before serving.

4 tablespoons unsalted butter
¼ cup all-purpose flour or white rice flour
1½ quarts Seafood Stock (page 36)
1 fresh mint sprig, plus more mint leaves for serving
Zest of 1 lemon
1 cup heavy cream
1½ pounds lump crabmeat
4 ounces Parmesan cheese, finely grated
Sea salt
Freshly ground black pepper

1 In a large pot, cook the butter and flour over medium heat for 2 minutes, whisking constantly until bubbling and thick.

2 Pour in the seafood stock, whisking to distribute the roux.

3 Add the mint sprig and lemon zest. Simmer for 5 minutes to thicken.

4 Add the heavy cream and simmer for 5 more minutes, then stir in the crab and simmer until heated through. Remove the pot from the heat and allow the soup to cool briefly.

5 Remove the mint sprig and stir in the Parmesan cheese. Season with salt and pepper. Garnish with fresh mint leaves to serve.

6 Chill, cover, and store any leftovers in the refrigerator for up to 2 days.

COOKING TIP: Always measure cheese before grating. Four ounces is equivalent to ½ cup, but once it is grated, it creates a fluffy pile that exceeds a full cup.

Nutritional Information Calories: 468; Saturated Fat: 19g; Carbohydrates: 11g; Sodium: 1247mg; Fiber: 0g; Protein: 38g

LOBSTER BISQUE

SERVES 4 TO 6 **PREP** 15 MINS **COOK** 1 HOUR

■ GLUTEN-FREE

If you're in the mood for soup but want something decadent and impressive, this lobster bisque fits the bill. It is so rich it needs nothing but a few Torn Baguette Croutons (page 197) and a glass of champagne to make a complete meal. Read the recipe a few times before you begin. It's not complicated, but it does require a few pots and it's helpful to have your ingredients cut and measured before you get started. Also, removing the lobster meat from the shell can be complicated, so you might want to review instructions or tutorials online.

2 live lobsters

4 tablespoons unsalted butter, divided

2 tablespoons olive oil

1 leek, white and pale green parts only, thinly sliced

1 onion, diced

1 celery stalk, diced

1 carrot, diced

6 garlic cloves, smashed

1 fresh thyme sprig

Sea salt

1 cup dry sherry or white wine

1 quart Seafood Stock (page 36)

2 tablespoons tomato paste

¼ teaspoon cayenne pepper

2 tablespoons all-purpose flour or sorghum flour

½ cup heavy cream

1 Bring a very large pot of water to boil. Plunge the lobsters into the water head first and cook for 8 minutes. Remove the cooked lobsters and place them on a cutting board to cool; reserve.

2 In a separate large pot over medium-low heat, melt 2 tablespoons of the butter with the olive oil and cook the leek, onion, celery, carrot, garlic, and thyme for 8 to 10 minutes, stirring frequently, until the vegetables have softened.

3 When the lobsters are cool enough to handle, remove the meat and place it in a bowl, reserving the shells.

4 Deglaze the pot of vegetables with the sherry and cook for 2 to 3 minutes, allowing some of the alcohol to evaporate.

5 Pour in the reserved lobster cooking liquid and the seafood stock. Stir in the tomato paste and cayenne pepper and bring to a simmer. Cook uncovered for 30 minutes, until the broth is reduced by about a third.

6 In a separate pot, whisk the remaining 2 tablespoons of butter with the flour over medium-low heat for about 10 minutes, until it turns amber in color.

7 Strain the lobster and vegetable broth through a fine-mesh sieve into a large bowl and pour it into the roux, whisking constantly. Simmer for 2 to 5 minutes until thickened.

8 Stir in the heavy cream and cook for 5 minutes. Stir in the reserved lobster meat and cook until heated through. Season with salt.

9 Enjoy immediately or chill, cover, and store in the refrigerator for up to 2 days.

COOKING TIP: If you object to steaming live lobsters, place them in the freezer for a couple of hours beforehand. Doing so puts them into a sleeplike state before plunging them into the boiling water.

Nutritional Information Calories: 471; Saturated Fat: 12g; Carbohydrates: 15g; Sodium: 1063mg; Fiber: 2g; Protein: 33g

NEW ENGLAND CLAM CHOWDER

SERVES 4 TO 6 **PREP** 15 MINS **COOK** 45 MINS

■ GLUTEN-FREE

Clam chowder will always be one of those dishes that warms me to my core, perhaps because I've enjoyed it when I've been shivering and wet. The year my husband and I started dating, he joined my family on our annual trip to Lummi Island. We all woke up in our tents surrounded by puddles of water. Fortunately, a little café on the island offered clam chowder. What a comfort! Don't worry though—you can enjoy this chowder rain or shine.

4 slices bacon, roughly chopped

4 celery stalks, finely diced

1 onion, finely diced

4 to 6 garlic cloves

Sea salt

1 quart Seafood Stock (page 36)

1 fresh thyme sprig

4 potatoes, peeled and diced

1 cup heavy cream

2 (6-ounce) cans clams, drained and roughly chopped

1 recipe Torn Baguette Croutons (page 197), for serving

1 In a large pot, cook the bacon over medium-low heat for 10 to 15 minutes, until it has rendered its fat and is nice and crispy. Transfer it to a paper towel.

2 Add the celery, onion, and garlic to the bacon fat in the pot and season with salt. Cook for 10 minutes until the vegetables are soft.

3 Add the stock and thyme and bring to a simmer. Add the potatoes and cook for 25 minutes, until tender.

4 Remove the thyme and discard. Remove about 2 cups of the broth and potatoes and purée until smooth. Return the purée to the pot and stir in the heavy cream. Bring to a simmer and cook for 5 minutes until thick.

continued

5 Stir in the clams and cook just until heated through. Ladle the soup into individual serving bowls and garnish with the cooked bacon and croutons.

6 Chill, cover, and store leftovers in the refrigerator for up to 2 days.

SUBSTITUTION TIP: If you want a dairy-free clam chowder, you're in luck! It works beautifully with coconut milk or coconut cream. To make the chowder without bacon, simply use butter or olive oil to cook the vegetables and stir in ½ teaspoon of liquid smoke seasoning during the last 2 minutes of cooking.

Nutritional Information Calories: 592; Saturated Fat: 14g; Carbohydrates: 61g; Sodium: 989mg; Fiber: 7g; Protein: 13g

MINORCAN CLAM CHOWDER

SERVES 4 TO 6 **PREP** 15 MINS **COOK** 30 MINS

■ PALEO ■ GLUTEN-FREE

Like Manhattan clam chowder, the Minorcan version is made with a tomato broth, but it also has a spicy kick from datil chiles. Legend has it that this pepper was brought to Florida in the 1700s by immigrants from the town of Minorca, Spain. Today, the majority of the peppers are produced in St. Augustine, Florida, but if you cannot find the traditional ingredient, use habanero instead.

2 tablespoons rendered bacon fat
1 onion, finely diced
4 to 6 garlic cloves
1 green bell pepper, finely diced
1 datil chile, minced
Sea salt
1 (28-ounce) can whole peeled tomatoes, hand crushed
1 quart Seafood Stock (page 36)
2 fresh thyme sprigs
1 teaspoon dried oregano
4 potatoes, peeled and diced
Freshly ground black pepper
2 (6-ounce) cans clams, drained and roughly chopped

1 In a large pot, melt the bacon fat over medium heat.

2 Add the onion, garlic, bell pepper, and chile to the pot and season with salt. Cook for 5 minutes until the vegetables are slightly softened.

3 Add the tomatoes, seafood stock, thyme, and oregano and bring to a simmer. Add the potatoes and cook for 25 minutes, until tender.

4 Remove the thyme sprig and discard. Season the soup with salt and pepper.

5 Stir in the clams and cook just until heated through.

6 Chill, cover, and store leftovers in the refrigerator for up to 2 days.

SUBSTITUTION TIP: If you prefer not to use bacon fat, feel free to use olive oil and add ½ teaspoon smoked paprika to the stock.

Nutritional Information Calories: 329; Saturated Fat: 3g; Carbohydrates: 56g; Sodium: 869mg; Fiber: 9g; Protein: 9g

SEAFOOD SOUPS & CHOWDERS

CREAM OF SCALLOP SOUP

SERVES 4 TO 6 **PREP** 15 MINS **COOK** 20 MINS

■ PALEO ■ GLUTEN-FREE ■ VEGAN ■ BIG 8 ALLERGEN–FRIENDLY

I adore the subtle flavor of scallops as they permeate this creamy soup. It's a great way to enjoy scallops without shelling out big bucks for the jumbo sea scallops. But if you can swing it, snag a few and pan sear them as a topping for this soup.

2 tablespoons unsalted butter
2 shallots, minced
Sea salt
1 pound bay scallops
3 tablespoons all-purpose flour
¼ cup dry white wine
1½ quarts Seafood Stock (page 36), heated
2 egg yolks
½ cup heavy cream

1 Melt the butter in a large pot over low heat. Add the shallots and a generous pinch of salt and cook for 10 minutes, stirring frequently, until the shallots are soft and fragrant.

2 Turn the heat up to medium. Add the scallops and cook for 1 to 2 minutes until heated through.

3 Whisk in the flour and cook for 2 minutes. Pour in the wine and sea-food stock all at once and cook for 2 minutes, until thickened slightly.

4 Purée the soup with an immersion blender. For a very smooth soup, pass through a china cap. Season with salt.

5 In a large bowl, beat together the egg yolks and heavy cream. Slowly whisk in 1 cup of the soup a few drops at a time to temper the eggs. Continue with the remaining soup until the eggs are completely integrated.

6 Return the soup to the pot and cook for another 2 minutes over medium-low heat to cook the egg yolks. Do not bring to a simmer.

7 Serve immediately or chill, cover, and refrigerate for 2 days. This soup is delicious served chilled, as well.

VARIATION TIP: For a beautiful entrée soup, purchase a dozen large sea scallops. Season generously with salt and pepper and sear in 2 tablespoons of butter in a hot skillet over medium-high heat. Place two to three scallops in the center of each bowl of soup.

Nutritional Information Calories: 286; Saturated Fat: 8g; Carbohydrates: 9g; Sodium: 475mg; Fiber: 0g; Protein: 24g

MUSSEL & POTATO SOUP

SERVES 4 TO 6 **PREP** 15 MINS **COOK** 35 MINS

■ GLUTEN-FREE

When I lived in England, fresh mussels were sold in nets along with various remnants of the ocean—small shells, pebbles, and seaweed. Although it wasn't the sterile presentation I was accustomed to, I loved feeling closer to the sea. Ultimately, I hope that I am constantly mindful of where my food comes from and capture that essence in every dish. The simplicity of this soup lets the fresh seafood shine. Enjoy with a few slices of crusty bread and butter.

2 tablespoons unsalted butter
2 tablespoons olive oil
1 yellow onion, diced
4 garlic cloves, minced
½ cup dry white wine
2 fresh thyme sprigs
1 quart Seafood Stock (page 36)
Sea salt
Freshly ground black pepper
4 potatoes, peeled and diced
½ cup heavy cream
2 to 3 pounds fresh mussels
1 cup roughly chopped fresh flat-leaf parsley, for serving

1 Scrub the mussels under cool running water and remove any bits of sand and the stringy "beard" that attaches to the inside of the mussel.

2 In a large pot, melt the butter with the olive oil and cook the onion and garlic over medium heat for 5 minutes.

3 Pour in the wine and cook for 2 minutes before adding the thyme and seafood stock. Season with salt and pepper.

4 Bring to a simmer and add the potatoes. Cook for 20 minutes uncovered, until the potatoes are soft.

5 Stir in the heavy cream and cook for 5 minutes.

6 Add the mussels, cover, and cook for 5 to 7 minutes, or until the mussels have opened. Discard any that have not opened after 10 minutes.

7 Ladle the soup into individual serving bowls and shower with fresh parsley.

8 Chill, cover, and store leftovers in the refrigerator for up to 2 days.

COOKING TIP: Always check mussels before cooking to ensure that all are tightly closed, or become so after they are tapped lightly, and shells are intact. Have your fishmonger do this for you before you purchase them—there's no sense wasting money on food that you'll have to toss.

Nutritional Information Calories: 570; Saturated Fat: 9g; Carbohydrates: 48g; Sodium: 960mg; Fiber: 6g; Protein: 35g

SALMON CHOWDER

SERVES 4 TO 6 **PREP** 15 MINS **COOK** 40 MINS

■ GLUTEN-FREE

In the Pacific Northwest, salmon is on the menu at nearly every restaurant, and honestly, I never got tired of it. I enjoy it smoked, cedar plank roasted, pan seared, fried, grilled, in a casserole, and especially in my mom's salmon chowder. Her version uses both raw salmon and smoked salmon for a nice blend of textures and flavors.

2 tablespoons unsalted butter
2 tablespoons olive oil
1 onion, finely diced
2 celery stalks, finely diced
4 potatoes, peeled and diced
1 teaspoon dried Italian herb blend
¼ teaspoon red chili flakes
1 quart Chicken Broth (page 32)
16 ounces salmon fillets, cut into
*   2-inch pieces*
1 cup heavy cream
8 ounces smoked salmon, flaked
Sea salt
Freshly ground black pepper

1 In a large pot, melt the butter with the olive oil over medium heat. Add the onion and celery and cook for 5 minutes, until slightly softened.

2 Add the potatoes, herb blend, and red chili flakes and cook for 2 to 3 minutes, until fragrant.

3 Pour in the chicken broth and bring to a simmer. Cover and cook for 20 minutes, until the potatoes are soft.

4 Stir in the raw salmon, cover, and poach for 5 minutes.

5 Stir in the heavy cream and smoked salmon and simmer gently for 5 minutes until the raw salmon is cooked through and the soup is thick and aromatic.

6 Season with salt and pepper.

7 Chill, cover, and store leftovers in the refrigerator for up to 2 days.

SUBSTITUTION TIP: You can use milk or half-and-half instead for this and other cream-based soups. Just remember, fat is stabilizing; the less fat in the dairy, the more susceptible it is to curdling at high temperatures, especially in the presence of acid.

Nutritional Information Calories: 605; Saturated Fat: 13g; Carbohydrates: 38g; Sodium: 1395mg; Fiber: 6g; Protein: 39g

SOUP & COMFORT

FINNAN HADDIE CHOWDER

SERVES 4 TO 6 **PREP** 10 MINS **COOK** 40 MINS

■ GLUTEN-FREE

Finnan Haddie is simply cold-smoked haddock, but it's more fun to say and it gives a nod to this soup's Scottish heritage. In northeast Scotland, Finnan Haddie is smoked using green wood and peat. Ideally, look for a good-quality, undyed smoked haddock for the best flavor.

1 cup heavy cream
1 quart Seafood Stock (page 36), divided
1 pound smoked haddock
2 tablespoons unsalted butter
1 onion, finely diced
2 celery stalks
2 garlic cloves
Sea salt
¼ cup dry sherry
1 bay leaf
1 fresh thyme sprig
4 potatoes, peeled and diced
*1 (6-ounce) can clams, drained and
   roughly chopped*
*¼ cup fresh chervil leaves, for serving
   (optional)*

1 In a large pot, heat the heavy cream, 1 cup of the seafood stock, and the smoked haddock over medium heat until it comes to the barest simmer. Remove from the heat and allow to steep.

2 In a separate large pot, melt the butter and add the onion, celery, and garlic. Season with salt and cook for 10 minutes until the vegetables are softened.

3 Pour in the sherry and cook for 2 minutes. Add the remaining 3 cups of stock, bay leaf, and thyme and bring to a simmer. Add the potatoes and cook for 25 minutes, until tender.

4 Remove the bay leaf and thyme and discard.

5 Strain the cream and stock mixture, pouring the liquid into the vegetables and placing the haddock on a cutting board. Flake the fish and discard bones and skin.

continued

SEAFOOD SOUPS & CHOWDERS

6 Bring the soup to a simmer and cook for 5 minutes.

7 Stir in the haddock and clams and cook just until heated through. Ladle the soup into individual serving bowls and garnish with chervil (if using).

8 Chill, cover, and store leftovers in the refrigerator for up to 2 days.

SUBSTITUTION TIP: If you wish to swap heavy cream for lighter options, such as whole milk, make a roux with 2 tablespoons of butter and 2 tablespoons of flour. Cook over medium-low heat until foamy and then whisk in the milk. Simmer until thickened. Pour this mixture into the soup at the very end.

Nutritional Information Calories: 488; Saturated Fat: 11g; Carbohydrates: 42g; Sodium: 1273mg; Fiber: 6g; Protein: 36g

BRAZILIAN FISH STEW

SERVES 4 TO 6 **PREP** 10 MINS **COOK** 20 MINS

■ PALEO ■ GLUTEN-FREE

Large pieces of wild fish can get pricey, but bargains can be found on fish ends and pieces. I snagged wild cod for a great price and created this tangy and spicy soup based on the classic Brazilian recipe. Don't skimp on the lime juice—it makes the soup!

1 tablespoon canola oil
1 onion, diced
2 garlic cloves, smashed
½ teaspoon red chili flakes
1 red bell pepper, cored and diced
1 green bell pepper, cored and diced
2 ripe tomatoes, cored and diced
1 tablespoon ground cumin
1 tablespoon smoked paprika
*2 cups Chicken Broth (page 32) or
   Roasted Vegetable Broth (page 29)*
1 cup coconut milk
Sea salt
*1½ pounds firm white fish fillets, cut into
   2-inch pieces*
*½ cup roughly chopped fresh cilantro,
   plus more for serving*
Juice of 2 limes
Lime wedges, for serving

1 In a large pot, heat the oil and cook the onion, garlic, and red chili flakes for 5 minutes over medium heat, until the vegetables are slightly softened.

2 Add the bell peppers, tomatoes, cumin, and paprika and cook for 2 minutes.

3 Pour in the broth and coconut milk and bring to a simmer for 5 minutes. Season with salt.

4 Add the fish to the pot, cover, and cook for 5 to 7 minutes or until the fish is opaque.

5 Stir in the cilantro and lime juice. Adjust the seasonings as necessary.

6 Serve with additional cilantro and lime wedges.

7 To store leftovers, cool, cover, and refrigerate for up to 2 days.

INGREDIENT TIP: Do you have leftover rice in your refrigerator? This is the perfect place to use it up. Simply stir it into the soup after the fish has cooked and allow it to cook for 1 minute, just until warmed.

Nutritional Information Calories: 399; Saturated Fat: 13g; Carbohydrates: 19g; Sodium: 113mg; Fiber: 5g; Protein: 33g

SEAFOOD SOUPS & CHOWDERS

FISH, RICE & FRESH TOMATO SOUP

SERVES 4 TO 6 **PREP** 10 MINS **COOK** 35 MINS

■ PALEO-FRIENDLY ■ GLUTEN-FREE

I often cook with canned tomatoes, but I made this soup during tomato season when I had just picked several pints of fresh heirloom cherry tomatoes. They were sweet and bursting off the vine as I picked them, seeds squirting everywhere. If you don't have access to cherry tomatoes, you can also use a can of diced tomatoes, though the flavor won't be quite as intense.

1 tablespoon olive oil
1 small onion, finely diced
2 carrots, finely diced
1 celery stalk, finely diced
4 garlic cloves, minced
½ teaspoon red chili flakes
1 teaspoon anchovy paste (optional)
2 cups roughly chopped cherry tomatoes
1½ quarts Chicken Broth (page 32) or Basic Vegetable Broth (page 28)
2 cups long-grain white rice
1½ pounds firm white fish, such as cod, cut into 2-inch pieces
¼ cup fresh lime juice
½ cup fresh cilantro
Lime wedges, for serving

1 Heat the olive oil in a large pot over medium-low heat. Add the onion, carrots, and celery and cook for 5 minutes or until the vegetables begin to soften.

2 Add the garlic, red chili flakes, and anchovy paste and cook for 1 minute.

3 Add the cherry tomatoes and cook for another 5 minutes until the tomatoes burst.

4 Pour in the broth and bring to a simmer. Add the rice, cover, and cook for 15 minutes; the rice will not yet be cooked through.

5 Add the fish, cover the pot, and cook for 5 to 10 minutes or until the fish is cooked through.

6 Stir in the lime juice and cilantro.

7 Serve immediately with lime wedges or chill, cover, and refrigerate leftovers for up to 2 days.

SUBSTITUTION TIP: To make this Paleo, simply omit the rice and reduce the broth to 1 quart.

Nutritional Information Calories: 610; Saturated Fat: 1g; Carbohydrates: 83g; Sodium: 428mg; Fiber: 4g; Protein: 50g

SEAFOOD SOUPS & CHOWDERS

135

TOM YUM SOUP
WITH SHRIMP

SERVES 4 **PREP** 10 MINS **COOK** 15 MINS

■ PALEO ■ GLUTEN-FREE

My husband's parents spent several weeks in Thailand and brought me back a small cookbook full of authentic Thai recipes. The book is full of personality and warmth, its frequent "alternative spellings" only adding to its charm. The flavors of its Tom Yum soup are absolutely spot-on and remind me of the best I've had in Thai restaurants. You can find all of the ingredients for this soup in an Asian market or online.

2 quarts Chicken Broth (page 32)
2 stalks lemongrass, halved and smashed with the broad side of a knife
2 (⅛-inch-thick) slices galangal root
4 to 6 kaffir lime leaves
2 Thai chiles, thinly sliced
1 onion, halved and thinly sliced
2 plum tomatoes, cored and diced
1 cup quartered button mushrooms
1 teaspoon sugar
2 tablespoons fish sauce
3 tablespoons fresh lime juice
1 teaspoon Thai chili paste
1 pound large shrimp, peeled and deveined
1 cup roughly chopped fresh cilantro
2 scallions, thinly sliced on a bias

1 In a large pot, bring the chicken broth to a simmer over medium heat. Add the lemongrass, galangal, lime leaves, and chiles. Cook for 2 to 3 minutes.

2 Stir in the onion, tomatoes, and mushrooms and cook for another 2 to 3 minutes.

3 Stir in the sugar, fish sauce, lime juice, and chili paste until dissolved, then add the shrimp. Cover the pot and cook for 5 minutes, until the shrimp is opaque and cooked through.

4 Stir in the cilantro and scallions just before serving.

5 To store leftovers, cool, cover, and refrigerate for up to 2 days.

SUBSTITUTION TIP: This soup is naturally light, but if you're looking for a few extra calories, replace 1 quart of the chicken broth with two cans of coconut milk.

Nutritional Information Calories: 158; Saturated Fat: 0g; Carbohydrates: 15g; Sodium: 936mg; Fiber: 2g; Protein: 26g

7

MEATY SOUPS,
STEWS & CHILI

BASIC BEEF STEW

SERVES 4 TO 6 **PREP** 10 MINS **COOK** 2 HOURS

■ PALEO-FRIENDLY ■ GLUTEN-FREE ■ BIG 8 ALLERGEN–FRIENDLY ■ FIX-AND-FORGET

I remember my mom making this stew in her slow cooker when I was young. We would come home to the delicious aromas of slow-cooked beef and vegetables permeating the house. Now I like to make it before I head out to surf for a day. When I walk in the door several hours later, sandy, suntanned, and totally mellow, nothing is quite as comforting as this dinner waiting for me.

2 tablespoons bacon fat
2½ pounds sirloin tip roast, cut into
    2-inch cubes
Sea salt
Freshly ground black pepper
1 cup fruity red wine, such as Zinfandel
1 cup Beef Stock (page 35)
2 tablespoons tomato paste
4 cubed white potatoes
4 carrots, cut into 2-inch pieces
1 yellow onion, sliced in eighths
1 rosemary sprig

FIX-AND-FORGET: To make this soup in a slow cooker, simply place all of the ingredients in a 4-quart slow cooker and cook on low for 6 hours or on high for 2 hours.

1 Preheat the oven to 325°F.

2 In a large Dutch oven, melt the bacon fat over medium-high heat. Pat the meat dry with paper towels and season generously with salt and pepper. Sear on all sides. You will likely need to do this in batches to not crowd the pot. Transfer the browned meat to a separate dish.

3 Deglaze the pan with the red wine, scraping up browned bits with a wooden spoon and allowing some of the alcohol to evaporate. Whisk in the stock and tomato paste. Return the meat to the pan and add the potatoes, carrots, onion, and rosemary. Give everything a good toss and season generously with salt and pepper.

4 Cover the pot, transfer it to the oven, and cook for 2 to 3 hours or until the meat is fork-tender.

5 Chill leftovers, cover, and store in the refrigerator for up to 3 days.

SUBSTITUTION TIP: To make this Paleo, use sweet potatoes instead of white potatoes.

Nutritional Information Calories: 816; Saturated Fat: 11g; Carbohydrates: 45g; Sodium: 381mg; Fiber: 8g; Protein: 81g

CHICKEN & WHITE WINE STEW

SERVES 4 TO 6 **PREP** 10 MINS **COOK** 40 MINS

■ GLUTEN-FREE

Whenever my husband is out of town, I love making delicious meat dishes. This one is so easy, I can set it on the stove top and entertain the kids until they're off to bed. Enjoyed with a glass of wine and a hunk of gluten-free bread, it's my idea of perfection.

2 tablespoons rendered bacon fat
2 pounds boneless, skinless chicken thighs, cut into 1-inch pieces
Sea salt
Freshly ground black pepper
1 onion, diced
2 garlic cloves, minced
1 cup dry white wine
1 quart Roasted Chicken Stock (page 31)
2 thyme sprigs
4 tablespoons cold unsalted butter

1 In a large pot, melt the bacon fat over medium heat. Season the chicken with salt and pepper and brown on all sides for about 5 minutes. Using a slotted spoon, transfer the chicken to a separate dish.

2 Cook the onion and garlic in the pot until they begin to soften, about 5 minutes. Deglaze the pan with white wine, scraping up the browned bits with a spoon. Add the chicken stock and thyme. Return the chicken to the pot. Cover and cook for 30 minutes, until the chicken is cooked through.

3 Remove the thyme sprigs from the pot and remove the pot from the heat. Stir in the butter, 1 tablespoon at a time, until well incorporated.

4 Chill, cover, and store leftovers in the refrigerator for up to 3 days.

COOKING TIP: If you prefer a more traditional coq au vin, use bone-in chicken pieces and add only 1 cup of chicken stock. Remove the chicken and reduce the sauce further before whisking in the butter.

Nutritional Information Calories: 660; Saturated Fat: 14g; Carbohydrates: 5g; Sodium: 375mg; Fiber: 1g; Protein: 67g

MEATY SOUPS, STEWS & CHILI

KALE, CANNELLINI BEAN & SAUSAGE SOUP

SERVES 4 TO 6 **PREP** 10 MINS **COOK** 30 MINS

■ GLUTEN-FREE ■ BIG 8 ALLERGEN–FRIENDLY

In one *Far Side* cartoon, two gorillas sit side by side and one remarks to the other, "You know, Sid, I really like bananas . . . I mean, I know that's not profound or nothin' . . . Heck! We ALL do . . . But for me, I think it goes much more beyond that." His sentiment sums up the way I feel about kale. I just can't get enough! But for the vegetable-averse, it's nice to pair it with a little meat, and Italian sausage does the trick.

*2 links mild Italian sausage,
    casings removed*

1 yellow onion, chopped

4 garlic cloves, minced

2 quarts Chicken Broth (page 32)

*2 (15-ounce) cans cannellini beans,
    drained and rinsed*

Sea salt

Freshly ground black pepper

*1 bunch Lacinato kale, ribs removed,
    leaves thinly sliced*

1 teaspoon red wine vinegar

1 In a large pot, break the sausage into pieces and cook over medium heat until browned. Add the onion and garlic and cook for another 5 minutes, until slightly softened.

2 Add the chicken broth and beans to the pot, season with salt and pepper, and bring the liquid to a simmer. Cook for 15 minutes or until the beans are heated through.

3 Stir in the kale and vinegar and cook for another 2 minutes, until the kale is wilted but still bright green.

4 Chill, cover, and store leftovers in the refrigerator for up to 3 days.

COOKING TIP: Want a spicier soup? Use hot Italian sausages and consider adding a pinch of red chili flakes to really turn up the heat.

Nutritional Information Calories: 281; Saturated Fat: 2g; Carbohydrates: 48g; Sodium: 771mg; Fiber: 14g; Protein: 18g

SOUP & COMFORT

142

CHICKEN MARSALA STEW

SERVES 4 TO 6 **PREP** 10 MINS **COOK** 30 MINS

■ GLUTEN-FREE

The caramel aroma and subtle, complex flavor of Marsala is so comforting to me, especially with mushrooms and fresh rosemary. Serve this with a loaf of crusty bread to sop up the delicious juices.

2 tablespoons olive oil

2 pounds boneless, skinless chicken thighs, trimmed of excess fat, cut into 2-inch pieces

Sea salt

Freshly ground black pepper

2 tablespoons all-purpose flour or white rice flour

1 onion, halved and thinly sliced

2 garlic cloves, smashed

2 tablespoons unsalted butter

2 cups thinly sliced cremini mushrooms

1 cup Marsala wine

1 quart Beef Stock (page 35)

1 rosemary sprig

1 In a large pot, heat the olive oil over medium heat. Season the chicken thoroughly with salt and pepper and lightly dust with the flour. Cook the chicken thighs until browned on the outside but not quite cooked through, about 5 minutes. Remove them with a slotted spoon to a separate dish.

2 Cook the onion and garlic in the pan until slightly softened, about 5 minutes. Push them to the sides of the pan and melt the butter in the center. Brown the mushrooms in 2 or 3 batches, pushing them to the side as you go.

3 Pour in the wine and beef stock and add the rosemary sprig. Return the chicken to the pot, cover, season with salt and pepper, and simmer for 20 minutes.

4 Chill, cover, and store leftovers in the refrigerator for up to 3 days.

COOKING TIP: Rosemary grows well in a wide variety of climates. Consider planting it in your yard so you have it available year-round!

Nutritional Information Calories: 644; Saturated Fat: 9g; Carbohydrates: 10g; Sodium: 700mg; Fiber: 1g; Protein: 69g

PORK & NAVY BEAN STEW

SERVES 4 TO 6 **PREP** 10 MINS **COOK** 1 HOUR, 15 MINS

■ PALEO ■ GLUTEN-FREE ■ BIG 8 ALLERGEN—FRIENDLY

Pork and beans served as the inspiration for this savory stew, but this version is more of a meal than a side dish. You can use any variety of canned beans you enjoy in this soup, just make sure to drain and rinse them before adding to the soup. Do not add dry beans directly to the soup because they will not cook in the presence of salt.

2 tablespoons olive oil

1 onion, diced

2 celery stalks, roughly chopped

2 carrots, roughly chopped

2 pounds boneless pork roast, cut into 1-inch pieces

Sea salt

Freshly ground black pepper

2 quarts Chicken Broth (page 32)

2 chipotles in adobo sauce, plus 1 tablespoon adobo sauce

¼ cup tomato paste

1 tablespoon packed brown sugar

2 (15-ounce) cans navy beans, drained and rinsed

1 teaspoon apple cider vinegar

8 ounces sour cream, for serving

1 cup fresh cilantro leaves, for serving

1 In a large pot, heat the olive oil and cook the onion, celery, and carrots for 5 minutes, until slightly softened.

2 Push the vegetables to the sides of the pot. Season the meat with salt and pepper and brown on all sides in the center of the pot, about 10 minutes total.

3 Pour in the chicken broth and add the chipotles, adobo, tomato paste, and brown sugar. Cover and cook for 1 hour, or until the pork is tender. Add the navy beans and vinegar and cook until just heated through. Adjust seasoning.

4 Serve with fresh sour cream and cilantro.

5 Chill, cover, and store leftovers in the refrigerator for up to 4 days.

INGREDIENT TIP: Always read the labels on canned goods to check for the presence of allergens. Some varieties of chipotles contain soybean oil and/or wheat.

Nutritional Information Calories: 821; Saturated Fat: 11g; Carbohydrates: 61g; Sodium: 1267mg; Fiber: 15g; Protein: 81g

OKTOBERFEST STEW
WITH APPLES, SAUSAGE & SWEET POTATOES

SERVES 4 TO 6 **PREP** 15 MINS **COOK** 45 MINS

■ PALEO ■ GLUTEN-FREE ■ VEGAN ■ BIG 8 ALLERGEN–FRIENDLY

My husband's parents lived in Germany and invited us to spend a few weeks with them over Christmas. Although Oktoberfest was done for the year, I enjoyed my first German bratwurst with a glass of mulled wine while listening to a brass band play under a light snowfall. German food, especially sausages, will forever hold a near and dear place in my heart. In this spirit, I bring Oktoberfest to you.

1 pound bratwurst sausages, cut into
   ½-inch slices
1 onion, halved and then sliced into
   thin circles
4 to 6 garlic cloves, smashed
3 apples, peeled, cored, and cut into
   8 wedges each
2 cups peeled, diced sweet potatoes
½ teaspoon ground cinnamon
Sea salt
Freshly ground black pepper
16 ounces hard cider
1 quart Roasted Chicken Stock (page 31)

1 In a large pot over medium heat, brown the sausages on each side, allowing them to render some fat, 5 to 7 minutes total. Transfer the sausages to a separate dish.

2 Cook the onion and garlic in the rendered fat for 5 minutes, being careful not to burn the garlic. Add the apples, sweet potatoes, and cinnamon. Season with salt and pepper. Cook for 2 minutes.

3 Pour in the hard cider and chicken stock, cover the pot, and cook for 15 minutes. Remove the lid and cook for another 15 to 20 minutes, until the sweet potatoes are soft. Allow to rest for 5 minutes before serving.

4 Chill leftovers, cover, and store in the refrigerator for up to 3 days.

SUBSTITUTION TIP: To make this vegan, replace the bratwurst with a mild vegan sausage and cook it in 1 tablespoon of olive oil. Replace the chicken stock with Roasted Vegetable Broth (page 29).

Nutritional Information Calories: 513; Saturated Fat: 11g; Carbohydrates: 37g; Sodium: 920mg; Fiber: 5g; Protein: 19g

SOUP & COMFORT

CHICKEN & SWEET PEPPER STEW

SERVES 4 TO 6 **PREP** 15 MINS **COOK** 1 HOUR

■ PALEO ■ GLUTEN-FREE ■ BIG 8 ALLERGEN–FRIENDLY

I love the sweetness of red and yellow bell peppers in this easy weeknight supper. Feel free to use chicken breasts if you wish, but the dark meat of the thighs stays nice and moist through the cooking time.

2 tablespoons olive oil

2 pounds boneless, skinless chicken thighs, trimmed of excess fat

Sea salt

Freshly ground black pepper

½ cup white wine

2 red bell peppers, cored and thinly sliced

2 yellow or orange bell peppers, cored and thinly sliced

1 onion, halved and thinly sliced

1 (15-ounce) can diced fire-roasted tomatoes

1 quart Chicken Broth (page 32)

1 teaspoon dried oregano

1 teaspoon smoked paprika

1 teaspoon red wine vinegar

1 Preheat the oven to 325°F.

2 Heat a Dutch oven over medium-high heat on the stove. Add the olive oil. Season the chicken with salt and pepper and sear on both sides until good and brown, about 5 minutes on each side.

3 Pour in the wine and add the bell peppers, onion, tomatoes, broth, oregano, paprika, and vinegar. Season generously with salt and pepper and give everything a good toss. Cover and place in the oven to cook for 45 minutes, until the chicken is cooked through and the vegetables have a soft stew-like consistency.

4 Allow to rest for 5 minutes before serving.

5 Chill leftovers, cover, and store in the refrigerator for up to 3 days.

INGREDIENT TIP: I prefer to use organic, free-range chicken because it has better flavor than conventionally raised chicken.

Nutritional Information Calories: 593; Saturated Fat: 6g; Carbohydrates: 16g; Sodium: 301mg; Fiber: 5g; Protein: 69g

VENISON STEW

SERVES 4 TO 6 **PREP** 10 MINS **COOK** 1 HOUR, 30 MINS

■ PALEO ■ GLUTEN-FREE ■ BIG 8 ALLERGEN—FRIENDLY ■ FIX-AND-FORGET

Venison does well with the long, slow cooking in this comforting stew. It's delicious in the cold winter months. You can also use beef stew meat if you're not a fan of the gaminess of venison.

2 tablespoons olive oil

2 pounds venison stew meat, cut into 2-inch pieces

Sea salt

Freshly ground black pepper

2 onions, cut into eight wedges each

4 celery stalks, diced

4 carrots, diced

6 garlic cloves, roughly chopped

1 cup dry red wine

1 (15-ounce) can whole peeled tomatoes, hand crushed

1 quart Beef Stock (page 35)

FIX-AND-FORGET: To make this soup in a slow cooker, brown the meat ahead of time for added flavor, or simply place all of the ingredients in a 4-quart slow cooker and cook on low for 6 hours or on high for 2 hours.

1 In a large pot, heat the olive oil over medium-high heat. Pat the meat dry with paper towels and season generously with salt and pepper. Brown the meat on all sides. You may have to do this in batches to avoid crowding the pan.

2 Add the onions, celery, carrots, and garlic to the pot and cook for 5 minutes, until slightly softened.

3 Deglaze the pan with wine and cook for a few minutes to evaporate some of the alcohol. Add the tomatoes and stock and bring to a simmer.

4 Cover and cook for 1 to 1½ hours or until the meat is tender. Adjust seasoning.

5 Chill, cover, and store leftovers in the refrigerator for up to 4 days.

INGREDIENT TIP: For a spicy twist, season the meat with 3 tablespoons of Creole seasoning blend before searing.

Nutritional Information Calories: 538; Saturated Fat: 3g; Carbohydrates: 21g; Sodium: 463mg; Fiber: 4g; Protein: 72g

MEXICAN BEAN & CHICKEN SOUP

SERVES 4 TO 6 **PREP** 10 MINS **COOK** 1 HOUR

■ GLUTEN-FREE ■ VEGAN ■ BIG 8 ALLERGEN–FRIENDLY ■ FIX-AND-FORGET

We once spent Christmas with Rich's family in Wyoming, where it snowed endlessly. His mom made two pots of this soup, one with meat and the other vegetarian for Rich. Whatever the weather, this soup is simple and delicious!

1 (15-ounce) can diced fire-roasted tomatoes
1 (15-ounce) can green enchilada sauce
1 (15-ounce) can black beans
1 (15-ounce) can kidney beans
16 ounces fresh or frozen and thawed corn kernels
1 tablespoon ground cumin
2 tablespoons dried oregano
6 garlic cloves, minced
1 onion, diced
1 pound chicken breast tenderloins
Sea salt
Freshly ground black pepper
8 ounces shredded Cheddar cheese, for serving
8 ounces sour cream, for serving

FIX-AND-FORGET: To make this soup in a slow cooker, simply place all of the ingredients (except those for serving) in a 4-quart slow cooker and cook on low for 6 hours or on high for 2 hours.

1 In a large pot, mix together the undrained cans of tomatoes, enchilada sauce, and beans. Add the corn, cumin, oregano, garlic, and onion and bring to a simmer over medium heat.

2 Add the chicken tenderloins to the pot and season generously with salt and pepper. Cover the pot and cook for 1 hour.

3 When they are fully cooked, remove the chicken tenderloins, cut them into bite-size pieces, and return them to the pot.

4 Ladle the soup into individual serving bowls and allow each person to garnish as desired with cheese and sour cream.

5 Chill, cover, and store leftovers in the refrigerator for up to 3 days.

SUBSTITUTION TIP: Simply omit the chicken to make this recipe vegan.

Nutritional Information Calories: 896; Saturated Fat: 20g; Carbohydrates: 72g; Sodium: 1309mg; Fiber: 20g; Protein: 71g

BEEF BOURGUIGNON

SERVES 4 TO 6 **PREP** 10 MINS **COOK** 2 TO 3 HOURS

■ PALEO ■ GLUTEN-FREE ■ BIG 8 ALLERGEN–FRIENDLY ■ FIX-AND-FORGET

Just before moving to Europe, I purchased *Mastering the Art of French Cooking* and followed Julia Child's recipe for beef bourguignon. It was delicious, of course, but I wanted to find a few shortcuts and less expensive ingredients to make it more accessible. At the end of the day, remember, you're cooking beef, mushrooms, and onions in wine—it's going to be good!

2 tablespoons rendered bacon fat

2½ pounds beef chuck roast, cut into 1-inch cubes

Sea salt

Freshly ground black pepper

2 tablespoons unsalted butter, divided

2 cups halved cremini mushrooms

1 onion, diced

1 garlic clove, smashed

¼ cup dry sherry or cognac (optional)

2 cups full-bodied red wine, such as Sangiovese

1 quart Chicken Broth (page 32)

2 tablespoons tomato paste

4 carrots, cut into 2-inch pieces

1 thyme sprig

1 bay leaf

1 In a large pot, heat the bacon fat over medium-high heat. Pat the meat dry with paper towels and season generously with salt and pepper. Sear on all sides. Do this in several batches to not crowd the pot. Remove browned meat to a separate dish.

2 Add 1 tablespoon of the butter to the pot. Brown the mushrooms in 2 or 3 batches, adding more butter as needed.

3 Add the onion and garlic and cook for 2 minutes.

4 Deglaze the pan with the sherry (if using), or simply add the red wine and whisk in the broth and tomato paste. Return the meat to the pan and add the carrots, thyme, and bay leaf. Give everything a good toss and season generously with salt and pepper.

5 Cover and simmer over low heat for 2½ to 3 hours, until the meat is falling apart. Remove the thyme and bay leaf and adjust seasoning.

6 Chill leftovers, cover, and store in the refrigerator for up to 3 days.

COOKING TIP: Although Beef Stock (page 35) can be used in this dish, I prefer the milder flavor of chicken broth. You could also use the Roasted Vegetable Broth (page 29) if that's what you have on hand.

Nutritional Information Calories: 908; Saturated Fat: 15g; Carbohydrates: 16g; Sodium: 546mg; Fiber: 3g; Protein: 97g

FIX-AND-FORGET: If you wish to make this soup in a slow cooker, brown the meat ahead of time for added flavor, or simply place all of the ingredients in a 4-quart slow cooker and cook on low for 6 hours or on high for 2 hours.

CHEESY CHICKEN ENCHILADA SOUP

SERVES 4 TO 6 **PREP** 10 MINS **COOK** 25 MINS

■ GLUTEN-FREE ■ VEGETARIAN

This cheesy, decadent soup is perfect for watching football and drinking beer on a Sunday afternoon. If you prefer a vegetarian version, simply omit the chicken and use Basic Vegetable Broth (page 28) or try the Black Bean & Spinach Enchilada Soup (page 188).

2 tablespoons olive oil
2 onions, thinly sliced
4 garlic cloves, minced
1 jalapeño pepper, minced
1 pound chicken tenderloins
1 tablespoon smoked paprika
1 teaspoon ground cumin
1 tablespoon ancho chili powder
1 (15-ounce) can diced fire-roasted tomatoes
1 quart Chicken Broth (page 32)
Sea salt
Freshly ground black pepper
4 cups shredded sharp Cheddar cheese, divided
1 cup fresh cilantro, for serving
8 ounces tortilla chips, for serving
1 avocado, peeled and diced, for serving

1 In a large pot, heat the olive oil and cook the onions, garlic, and jalapeño pepper over medium heat for 5 minutes. Push the vegetables to the side and sear the chicken until it is browned on all sides, about 5 minutes. The chicken will not be cooked through.

2 Add the paprika, cumin, chili powder, tomatoes, and chicken broth, season with salt and pepper, and bring to a simmer for 10 minutes.

3 Remove the pot from the heat and stir in 3½ cups of the cheese. Stir until melted.

4 To serve, ladle the soup into individual serving bowls and garnish with the remaining ½ cup of cheese, fresh cilantro, tortilla chips, and avocado.

COOKING TIP: If you're faint of heart when it comes to spices, remove the seeds and membranes from the jalapeño and start with half of the pepper or even less.

Nutritional Information Calories: 1028; Saturated Fat: 28g; Carbohydrates: 45g; Sodium: 1715mg; Fiber: 11g; Protein: 76g

SOUP & COMFORT

SPICY CHICKEN & SWEET POTATO CHOWDER

SERVES 4 TO 6 **PREP** 10 MINS **COOK** 30 MINS

■ GLUTEN-FREE

Sweet potatoes are my favorite starchy vegetable. They're sweet, creamy, filling, loaded with nutrients, and beautiful in color, adding depth and richness to this flavorful chowder. Enjoy them in all their glory.

2 tablespoons olive oil

1 onion, diced

4 garlic cloves, minced

1 red bell pepper, cored and diced

1 pound boneless, skinless chicken breasts, cut into 1-inch pieces

1 quart Chicken Broth (page 32)

2 cups peeled and diced sweet potatoes

2 cups fresh corn kernels

½ cup fire-roasted green chiles

1 teaspoon ground cumin

1 teaspoon smoked paprika

¼ teaspoon cayenne pepper

Sea salt

Freshly ground black pepper

½ cup heavy cream

1 Heat the oil in a large pot over medium heat, add the onion, garlic, and bell pepper, and cook for 5 minutes or until the vegetables begin to soften.

2 Push the vegetables to the side and cook the chicken for 5 minutes, stirring constantly, until lightly browned. Add the broth, sweet potatoes, corn kernels, chiles, cumin, paprika, and cayenne pepper. Season generously with salt and pepper. Bring to a simmer, cover, and cook for 15 minutes, until the sweet potatoes are just cooked.

3 Stir in the heavy cream and cook for 5 more minutes.

4 Chill, cover, and store leftovers in the refrigerator for up to 2 days.

INGREDIENT TIP: Feel free to use frozen corn kernels in this recipe. Simply defrost before adding to the soup.

Nutritional Information Calories: 524; Saturated Fat: 7g; Carbohydrates: 45g; Sodium: 328mg; Fiber: 6g; Protein: 38g

MEATY SOUPS, STEWS & CHILI

GROUND BEEF & KIDNEY BEAN CHILI

SERVES 4 TO 6 **PREP** 15 MINS **COOK** 35 MINS

■ GLUTEN-FREE ■ BIG 8 ALLERGEN–FRIENDLY

I have been making this chili for years with beef chuck but replaced it with ground beef in this recipe and absolutely loved the results. The flavor of the meat permeates the stew, so purchase good-quality grass-fed beef if you're able to.

1½ pounds ground beef

Sea salt

Freshly ground black pepper

2 onions, diced

4 carrots, diced

2 celery stalks, diced

2 red bell peppers, cored and thinly sliced

2 (15-ounce) cans diced fire-roasted tomatoes

1 (15-ounce) can kidney beans, drained and rinsed

1 tablespoon ancho chili powder

1 tablespoon smoked paprika

1 tablespoon ground cumin

1 teaspoon ground cinnamon

¼ teaspoon curry powder (optional)

¼ teaspoon cayenne pepper

1 Heat a large pot over medium–high heat. Season the meat with salt and pepper and place it in the heated pot to brown for 5 to 10 minutes, stirring occasionally.

2 Add the onion, carrots, celery, and bell peppers and cook for another 5 minutes, until slightly softened.

3 Stir in the tomatoes, beans, chili powder, paprika, cumin, cinnamon, curry powder (if using), and cayenne pepper and cook for 30 minutes, to allow the vegetables to soften further and all of the flavors to come together.

4 To serve, ladle the chili into individual serving bowls. Chill, cover, and store leftovers in the refrigerator for up to 4 days.

COOKING TIP: Grind your own beef for the best texture and flavor. I have a meat grinder attachment for my KitchenAid mixer that works wonders with all kinds of meats. To make this Paleo, simply omit the kidney beans and increase the beef by ½ pound.

Nutritional Information Calories: 529; Saturated Fat: 4g; Carbohydrates: 41g; Sodium: 405mg; Fiber: 13g; Protein: 62g

BEEF STOUT STEW
WITH HERBED DUMPLINGS

SERVES 4 TO 6 **PREP** 15 MINS **COOK** 2 HOURS, 45 MINS

■ GLUTEN-FREE

This hearty stew is perfect in the fall after a long hike or your last garden clean-up of the season. Make sure to use a good-quality stout from a craft brewery. Being from Portland, I'm partial to Bridgeport beers. Dark holiday beers such as Jubelale are also delicious in this stew.

FOR THE STEW

2 tablespoons rendered bacon fat

2½ pounds beef chuck roast, cut into 1-inch cubes

Sea salt

Freshly ground black pepper

1 onion, diced

4 carrots, diced

2 garlic cloves, smashed

12 ounces stout beer

1 quart Chicken Broth (page 32)

2 tablespoons tomato paste

1 bay leaf

FOR THE DUMPLINGS

1½ cups all-purpose flour

1 teaspoon baking powder

½ teaspoon baking soda

¼ teaspoon sea salt

4 tablespoons unsalted butter, at room temperature

½ cup milk

1 teaspoon minced fresh thyme

1 tablespoon minced fresh flat-leaf parsley

1 In a large pot, heat the bacon fat over medium-high heat. Pat the meat dry with paper towels and season generously with salt and pepper. Sear on all sides. Do this in several batches to not crowd the pot. Transfer the browned meat to a separate dish.

2 Add the onion, carrots, and garlic to the pot and cook for 2 minutes.

3 Deglaze the pan with the beer. Add the broth, tomato paste, and bay leaf. Return the meat to the pan and give everything a good toss. Season generously with salt and pepper.

4 Cover the pot and simmer over low heat for 2½ hours, until the meat is tender.

5 While the stew is cooking, make the dumplings. Mix together the flour, baking powder, baking soda, and sea salt in a small mixing bowl. Add the butter, milk, thyme, and parsley and whisk to mix thoroughly.

6 Drop the dumplings into the stew by the spoonful and cook for 10 to 15 minutes or until they are cooked through.

7 Allow the stew to rest for 10 minutes before serving.

8 Chill leftovers, cover, and store in the refrigerator for up to 3 days.

SUBSTITUTION TIP: This stew is just as good with a quality gluten-free dark beer and dumplings made with gluten-free flour. Actually, I think gluten-free flours make a softer dumpling than wheat flour.

Nutritional Information Calories: 1049; Saturated Fat: 19g; Carbohydrates: 52g; Sodium: 710mg; Fiber: 4g; Protein: 102g

MOROCCAN CHICKEN STEW

SERVES 4 TO 6 **PREP** 15 MINS **COOK** 1 HOUR

■ PALEO ■ GLUTEN-FREE ■ BIG 8 ALLERGEN–FRIENDLY

My friend Anna introduced me to cooking chicken with citrus, curry, and paprika. The flavors are bright and complex with just a hint of spice. When preparing lemon zest, make sure not to include the white pith, which will impart a bitter flavor to the stew.

2 tablespoons olive oil
1 whole chicken, cut into pieces
Sea salt
Freshly ground black pepper
1 onion, halved and thinly sliced
1 teaspoon minced fresh ginger
4 garlic cloves, smashed
2 carrots, cut into 2-inch pieces
2 celery stalks, roughly chopped
¼ cup white wine
1 quart Chicken Broth (page 32)
Zest of 1 lemon, cut into long strips
2 tablespoons curry powder
1 tablespoon smoked paprika
1 cup mixed pitted olives (optional)
1 cup toasted sliced almonds, for serving

1 Preheat the oven to 325°F.

2 In a Dutch oven or a large cast-iron skillet fitted with a lid, heat the olive oil over medium-high heat on the stove. Season the chicken with salt and pepper and brown on all sides, for about 10 minutes total. Remove the chicken to a separate plate.

3 Cook the onion, ginger, garlic, carrots, and celery for 5 minutes.

4 Pour in the wine and broth and add the lemon zest, curry powder, paprika, and olives (if using). Season generously with salt and pepper and give everything a good toss. Cover and place in the oven to cook for 45 minutes, until the meat is cooked through.

5 Allow to rest for 5 minutes before serving. Garnish with the sliced almonds.

6 Chill leftovers, cover, and store in the refrigerator for up to 3 days.

SUBSTITUTION TIP: To keep this allergen-free, simply omit the almonds.

Nutritional Information Calories: 497; Saturated Fat: 5g; Carbohydrates: 17g; Sodium: 412mg; Fiber: 7g; Protein: 39g

PORK CHILI VERDE

SERVES 4 TO 6 **PREP** 10 MINS **COOK** 2 HOURS

■ PALEO ■ GLUTEN-FREE ■ BIG 8 ALLERGEN–FRIENDLY

Tomatillos look like small green tomatoes covered in husks. But their flavor is bright and zingy and makes this tangy soup unique and delicious. Serve with big hunks of cornbread and a generous dollop of sour cream and fresh cilantro.

2 onions, cut into thin rings
4 cups halved tomatillos
4 garlic cloves, unpeeled
1 to 2 jalapeño peppers,
  halved lengthwise
3 tablespoons olive oil, divided
Sea salt
Freshly ground black pepper
2 pounds boneless pork roast, cut into
  1-inch pieces
2 quarts Chicken Broth (page 32)
1 tablespoon ground cumin
1 teaspoon ancho chili powder
Juice of 2 limes
1 cup fresh cilantro leaves, for serving

COOKING TIP: To save time, you can purchase 16 ounces of good-quality salsa verde instead of roasting the tomatillos, onions, garlic, and jalapeño.

Nutritional Information Calories: 518; Saturated Fat: 4g; Carbohydrates: 20g; Sodium: 424mg; Fiber: 5g; Protein: 64g

1 Preheat the oven to 350°F.

2 In a baking dish, spread out the onions, tomatillos, garlic, and jalapeño pepper. Toss with 2 table-spoons of the olive oil and season generously with salt and pepper. Roast uncovered for 30 minutes, until the vegetables are just beginning to brown.

3 In a large pot, heat the remaining 1 tablespoon of oil over medium heat and brown the pork. Add the chicken broth, cumin, and chili powder and bring to a simmer. Season with salt and pepper.

4 When the onion and tomatillo mixture has finished cooking, let it cool briefly and then transfer it to a blender and pulse a few times for a chunky sauce. Add this to the pot, cover, and cook for 1 to 2 hours, until the pork is tender.

5 Stir in the lime juice, shower with fresh cilantro, and adjust the season-ings as necessary.

6 Chill, cover, and store leftovers in the refrigerator for up to 4 days.

INDIAN CHICKEN
IN SPICED COCONUT MILK

SERVES 4 TO 6 **PREP** 15 MINS **COOK** 25 MINS

■ PALEO ■ GLUTEN-FREE

I can always tell when my neighbors are cooking because the pungent aromas of Indian food permeate my apartment. The intoxicating fragrance finally got the better of me one morning and I raced to the Asian market to grab some spices and make my own curry. If you cannot find all of the ingredients, don't worry, it will still taste amazing if you are missing one or two. This soup is delicious with steamed rice or the Indian flat bread *naan*.

2 tablespoons coriander seeds
2 teaspoons cumin seeds
12 fresh curry leaves
4 dried chiles, stems removed
2 tablespoons coconut oil
2 onions, halved and thinly sliced
4 garlic cloves, minced
1 teaspoon tamarind concentrate
1 teaspoon ground turmeric
2 (15-ounce) cans coconut milk
1 quart Chicken Broth (page 32)
  shredded chicken meat
1 pound green beans, cut into
  1-inch pieces
Sea salt
Freshly ground black pepper
Juice of 1 lime

1 In a dry skillet over medium heat, toast the coriander and cumin seeds until fragrant, about 2 minutes. Shake the pan constantly to prevent scorching.

2 Add the curry leaves and toast for another 2 minutes, until curled and darkened.

3 Add the chiles and press into the pan to toast for about 1 minute on each side.

4 Remove the pan from the heat and allow the spices to cool, then place them in a spice grinder and pulse until finely ground.

5 In a large pot, heat the coconut oil and cook the onion and garlic for 5 minutes, until slightly softened. Add the ground spices and cook for 2 to 3 minutes.

6 Add the tamarind, turmeric, coconut milk, and broth and bring to a simmer for 15 minutes. Stir in the chicken meat and green beans and cook for about 5 minutes, until the beans are bright green and the chicken is heated through. Season with salt and pepper and stir in the lime juice.

SUBSTITUTION TIP: If you cannot find tamarind, use 1 teaspoon of tomato paste mixed with 1 tablespoon of lime juice.

Nutritional Information Calories: 876; Saturated Fat: 51g; Carbohydrates: 30g; Sodium: 250mg; Fiber: 10g; Protein: 57g

CUBAN-STYLE CHICKEN STEW

SERVES 4 TO 6 **PREP** 10 MINS, PLUS 1 HOUR TO MARINATE **COOK** 45 MINS

■ PALEO ■ GLUTEN-FREE ■ BIG 8 ALLERGEN–FRIENDLY

Now that the embargo has been softened, I'm so eager to hop on a plane to Cuba. It's filled with so much lore and mystery in the minds of Americans, but I think the food alone could tempt me. This stew includes several classic Cuban ingredients, which are easy to find in any grocery store. White rice is a nice side, but the stew already contains potatoes, so it's not essential.

Zest and juice of 1 lime
Zest and juice of 1 orange
4 garlic cloves, minced
1 teaspoon ground cumin
1 teaspoon dried oregano
5 tablespoons olive oil, divided
2 pounds bone-in skin-on chicken thighs
Sea salt
Freshly ground black pepper
1 green bell pepper, cored and thinly sliced
1 onion, halved and thinly sliced
½ cup dry white wine
4 cups peeled and diced white potatoes
1 cup frozen peas, defrosted
2 tablespoons tomato paste
2 cups Chicken Broth (page 32)
¼ cup raisins
⅓ cup pepper-stuffed olives
2 tablespoons capers
2 tablespoons fresh flat-leaf parsley, for serving

1 In a large nonreactive bowl, mix the lime and orange zest and juices with the garlic, cumin, oregano, and 4 tablespoons of olive oil. Coat the chicken thighs in this mixture and place in the refrigerator to marinate for at least 1 hour.

2 Remove the chicken from the marinade and pat dry. Season generously with salt and pepper.

3 In a large pot, heat the remaining 1 tablespoon of olive oil over medium heat. Sear the chicken on both sides in the oil. Remove to a separate plate to rest.

4 Cook the pepper and onion in the pot for 5 minutes, until slightly softened. Deglaze the pan with white wine and add the potatoes, peas, tomato paste, and chicken broth. Return the chicken to the pot, cover, and cook for 30 minutes, until the chicken is cooked through and the potatoes are soft.

5 Add the raisins, olives, and capers and cook for another 5 minutes. Adjust the seasonings as necessary. Shower with the fresh parsley.

6 Chill, cover, and store leftovers in the refrigerator for up to 4 days.

COOKING TIP: This dish is traditionally made with bone-in chicken pieces. While that does ensure the chicken stays moist and flavorful, I find the soup is easier for children and dinner guests to enjoy with boneless pieces of meat.

Nutritional Information Calories: 756; Saturated Fat: 10g; Carbohydrates: 46g; Sodium: 528mg; Fiber: 9g; Protein: 37g

VIETNAMESE BEEF STEW

SERVES 4 TO 6 **PREP** 10 MINS **COOK** 2 HOURS

■ PALEO-FRIENDLY ■ GLUTEN-FREE ■ BIG 8 ALLERGEN–FRIENDLY ■ FIX-AND-FORGET

Every culture that eats beef seems to have at least one recipe for turning tough cuts of meat into something tender and succulent. I make no claims to the authenticity of this recipe, but I will stand by the flavors!

2 tablespoons canola oil
2½ pounds beef chuck roast, cut into 2-inch cubes
Sea salt
Freshly ground black pepper
1 teaspoon Chinese five-spice powder
1 quart Beef Stock (page 35)
1 tablespoon soy sauce
1 tablespoon rice wine vinegar
2 tablespoons tomato paste
4 carrots, cut into 2-inch pieces
1 yellow onion, sliced in eighths
4 garlic cloves, roughly chopped
1 Thai chile, halved lengthwise
1 cinnamon stick
1 lemongrass spear, white and pale green parts only, halved
2 kaffir lime leaves

1 Preheat the oven to 325°F.

2 In a large Dutch oven, heat the oil over medium-high heat.

3 Pat the meat dry with paper towels and season generously with salt, pepper, and the five-spice powder. Sear on all sides. You will likely need to do this in batches to not crowd the pot. Transfer the browned meat to a separate dish.

4 Deglaze the pan with the beef stock and whisk in the soy sauce, rice wine vinegar, and tomato paste. Return the meat to the pan and add the carrots, onion, garlic, chile, cinnamon, lemongrass, and lime leaves.

5 Give everything a good toss and season generously with salt and pepper.

6 Cover the pot, transfer it to the oven, and braise for 2 to 3 hours or until the meat is fork-tender.

7 Chill leftovers, cover, and store in the refrigerator for up to 3 days.

FIX-AND-FORGET: To make this soup in a slow cooker, brown the meat ahead of time for added flavor and then . place all of the ingredients (except the fresh herbs) in a 4-quart slow cooker and cook on low for 6 hours or on high for 2 hours.

COOKING TIP: For Paleo, gluten-free, and allergen-free stew, omit the soy sauce or use coconut aminos or gluten-free soy sauce.

Nutritional Information Calories: 733; Saturated Fat: 9g; Carbohydrates: 12g; Sodium: 558mg; Fiber: 3g; Protein: 96g

SOUP & COMFORT

SPICY CHICKEN PEANUT STEW

SERVES 4 TO 6 **PREP** 10 MINS **COOK** 20 MINS

■ PALEO ■ GLUTEN-FREE ■ VEGAN

This soup reminds me of peanut sauce used for stir-fries and for dipping salad rolls. I can never get enough of the sauce. Well, I couldn't until I made this soup. Once you try it, you'll know what I mean.

2 tablespoons olive oil
1 onion, diced
1 tablespoon minced fresh ginger
1 tablespoon minced garlic
1 cup natural peanut butter
1 teaspoon minced lemongrass
1 quart Chicken Broth (page 32) with
    shredded chicken meat
2 cups roasted peanuts, roughly chopped
½ teaspoon cayenne pepper
Sea salt
Freshly ground black pepper
2 tablespoons fresh lime juice
1 cup fresh basil leaves, roughly chopped
1 cup fresh cilantro leaves,
    roughly chopped

1 In a large pot, heat the olive oil over medium heat. Cook the onion, ginger, and garlic until fragrant and soft, about 5 minutes. Add the peanut butter to the pot and stir until it has melted completely.

2 Add the lemongrass, broth, chicken, peanuts, and cayenne. Season with salt and pepper.

3 Simmer for 15 minutes until slightly thickened.

4 Stir in the lime juice just before serving and garnish with fresh basil and cilantro.

5 Chill, cover, and store leftovers in the refrigerator for 3 days.

INGREDIENT TIP: If you live near an Asian market, try to find some fresh Thai basil to top this soup.

Nutritional Information Calories: 909; Saturated Fat: 12g; Carbohydrates: 31g; Sodium: 123mg; Fiber: 11g; Protein: 41g

8

VEGETARIAN
SOUPS & STEWS

BUTTERNUT SQUASH & CAULIFLOWER CURRY
WITH COCONUT YOGURT

SERVES 4 TO 6 **PREP** 10 MINS **COOK** 30 TO 40 MINS

■ PALEO ■ GLUTEN-FREE ■ VEGAN

In England, I loved that Indian food was present in nearly every pub; even deep in the countryside, you could find tikka masala. It was a bright spot in the cold, dreary English winter. Here's a vegan version that's a cinch to prepare. Authentic? No, not really. Delicious? You bet!

1 two-pound butternut squash, peeled and cut into 2-inch pieces, about 4 cups total
1 cauliflower head, broken into florets
1 red onion, halved and thinly sliced
2 tablespoons curry powder
1 (15-ounce) can diced fire-roasted tomatoes
1 quart Basic Vegetable Broth (page 28)
1 teaspoon garam masala
1 tablespoon apple cider vinegar
Sea salt
Freshly ground black pepper
6 to 8 ounces plain coconut yogurt, for serving
1 cup fresh cilantro leaves, for serving

1 In a large pot over medium heat, mix together the squash, cauliflower, onion, curry powder, tomatoes, broth, and garam masala. Season with salt and pepper.

2 Bring the liquid to a simmer, cover the pot, and cook for 30 to 40 minutes or until the squash is tender.

3 Adjust the seasonings as necessary. Ladle the soup into individual serving bowls, drizzle each serving with some of the yogurt, and garnish with fresh cilantro.

4 Chill, cover, and store leftovers in the refrigerator for up to 4 days.

Nutritional Information Calories: 194; Saturated Fat: 2g; Carbohydrates: 38g; Sodium: 165mg; Fiber: 8g; Protein: 9g

SMOKY SPLIT PEA SOUP

SERVES 4 TO 6 **PREP** 10 MINS **COOK** 1 HOUR TO 1 HOUR, 30 MINS

■ GLUTEN-FREE ■ VEGAN ■ BIG 8 ALLERGEN–FRIENDLY ■ FIX-AND-FORGET

Ham and bacon aren't the only foods with a delicious smokiness, so I wanted to come up with a vegetarian version of the classic soup that even my husband and vegetarian friends can enjoy. Here it is for you to enjoy as well.

1 onion, diced

1 celery stalk, diced

1 carrot, diced

1½ cups green split peas

1½ quarts Basic Vegetable Broth (page 28)

2 teaspoons smoked paprika

½ teaspoon smoked sea salt (optional) or regular sea salt

FIX-AND-FORGET: To make this soup in a slow cooker, simply place all of the ingredients in a 4-quart slow cooker and cook on low for 4 hours or on high for 1 hour and 30 minutes.

1 In a large pot over medium-low heat, mix together the onion, celery, carrot, peas, broth, paprika, and sea salt. Bring the liquid to a simmer, cover the pot, and cook for 1 to 1½ hours, until the peas and vegetables are soft.

2 To store, chill, cover, and refrigerate for up to 3 days.

INGREDIENT TIP: You can also use liquid smoke seasoning to impart a delicious flavor to this soup and to vegan chowders. Just remember, a little smoke goes a long way!

Nutritional Information Calories: 293; Saturated Fat: 0g; Carbohydrates: 53g; Sodium: 400mg; Fiber: 21g; Protein: 19g

ROASTED GARLIC & 10-BEAN SOUP
WITH BALSAMIC REDUCTION

SERVES 4 TO 6 **PREP** 10 MINS **COOK** 30 MINS

■ GLUTEN-FREE ■ VEGAN ■ BIG 8 ALLERGEN–FRIENDLY

I had never used 10-bean soup mix before crafting this recipe. Initially, I thought it was strange to combine several types of beans that require different soaking and cooking times. But it actually works beautifully. The softer legumes, such as lentils and black-eyed peas, virtually disintegrate into the soup for a nice, creamy base.

2 cups 10-bean soup mix
2 quarts water
1 head roasted garlic
2 tablespoons olive oil, divided
1 quart Roasted Vegetable Broth
    (page 29)
1 onion, minced
2 celery stalks, minced
2 carrots, minced
1 fresh rosemary sprig
Sea salt
Freshly ground black pepper
1 cup balsamic vinegar

1 Place the beans in a large container and cover with three times the volume of water, about 6 to 8 cups. Soak overnight at room temperature.

2 Drain and rinse the beans. In a large pot, bring the water to a boil and add the beans. Reduce the heat to low and simmer, uncovered, for 1 hour or until the beans and tender. Drain the beans.

3 In a large pot over medium heat, mix the cooked beans with the garlic, olive oil, broth, onion, celery, carrots, and rosemary. Season with salt and pepper. Cover and cook for 30 minutes, until the vegetables are soft.

4 Meanwhile, in a separate saucepan, reduce the balsamic vinegar over low heat until thick and syrupy, about 15 minutes. Set aside.

5 When the soup has finished cooking, remove the rosemary, then transfer 4 cups of the soup to a blender and purée until smooth. Pour it back into the pot and stir to mix thoroughly. Adjust the seasonings as necessary.

6 To serve, ladle the soup into individual serving bowls and drizzle with the balsamic reduction.

7 Chill, cover, and store leftovers in the refrigerator for up to 3 days.

COOKING TIP: To save time, soak and cook the beans a day ahead of time so you have minimal work the day you want to prepare this soup.

Nutritional Information Calories: 291; Saturated Fat: 1g; Carbohydrates: 61g; Sodium: 331mg; Fiber: 32g; Protein: 19g

CILANTRO POTATO SOUP

SERVES 4 TO 6 **PREP** 10 MINS **COOK** 20 MINS

■ GLUTEN-FREE ■ VEGAN ■ BIG 8 ALLERGEN–FRIENDLY

My neighbor Ludy is a vegetarian and shared this recipe for simple potato soup. She serves it with her homemade fiery chile de arbol salsa and corn tortilla chips.

1 quart Basic Vegetable Broth (page 28)
1 bunch fresh cilantro, roughly chopped, divided
1 bunch scallions, roughly chopped, divided
Sea salt
Freshly ground black pepper
6 cups peeled and diced potatoes
Tortilla chips, for serving
Fire-roasted salsa, for serving

1 In a large pot over medium heat, mix together the vegetable broth, half of the cilantro, and half of the scallions. Bring the broth to a simmer, season generously with salt and pepper, and cook for 5 minutes.

2 Carefully add the diced potatoes to the pot and simmer, uncovered, for 15 minutes or until the potatoes are tender.

3 Shower the soup with the remaining cilantro and scallions and serve with chips and hot salsa.

4 Chill, cover, and store leftovers in the refrigerator for up to 3 days.

PAIRING TIP: This soup is best enjoyed as an appetizer. For a complete meal, serve with cheese quesadillas and a big bowl of fresh guacamole.

Nutritional Information Calories: 193; Saturated Fat: 0g; Carbohydrates: 43g; Sodium: 224mg; Fiber: 7g; Protein: 5g

BAKED POTATO SOUP

SERVES 4 TO 6 **PREP** 15 MINS **COOK** 20 MINS

■ GLUTEN-FREE ■ VEGETARIAN

My mother-in-law, Debbie, makes this soup and a loaf of homemade wheat bread every Christmas Eve. Originally, the soup contained crisp cooked bacon, but since Rich stopped eating meat, she makes a vegetarian version so everyone can enjoy it. That means you can, too. I was thrilled when Debbie sent me the recipe to include in this book.

4 tablespoons unsalted butter
1 yellow onion, diced
1 carrot, sliced
1 celery stalk, sliced
4 medium potatoes, diced
¼ cup all-purpose flour
1 quart Basic Vegetable Broth (page 28)
Sea salt
Freshly ground black pepper
½ cup heavy cream
2 cups shredded sharp Cheddar
2 scallions, thinly sliced on a bias,
  for serving
Sour cream, for serving

1 In a large pot, melt the butter over medium heat. Add the onion, carrot, and celery and cook for 5 minutes, until slightly softened. Add the potato and cook for 2 to 3 minutes.

2 Sprinkle in the flour and stir until it coats the vegetables and soaks up the butter. Pour in the vegetable broth, season with salt and pepper, and bring to a simmer for 5 minutes.

3 Pour in the heavy cream and simmer until thick. Remove the pot from the heat and allow to rest for 5 minutes.

4 Stir in the grated cheese until melted.

5 To serve, garnish each portion of soup with scallions and a dollop of cold sour cream.

6 Chill, cover, and store leftovers in the refrigerator for up to 3 days.

SUBSTITUTION TIP: To make this gluten-free, use a gluten-free flour alternative such as sorghum flour or white rice flour.

Nutritional Information Calories: 457; Saturated Fat: 13g; Carbohydrates: 48g; Sodium: 591mg; Fiber: 7g; Protein: 19g

CORN CHOWDER
WITH PICKLED JALAPEÑOS

SERVES 4 TO 6 **PREP** 10 MINS **COOK** 1 HOUR

■ GLUTEN-FREE ■ VEGETARIAN ■ VEGAN

I enjoyed corn chowder for the first time at a restaurant in Phoenix on my thirtieth birthday. I begged the server for the recipe and he conceded. The recipe was written for the restaurant dinner rush, but after a little basic math and some trial and error, I adapted it into the most delicious corn chowder you'll ever taste.

2 jalapeño peppers, thinly sliced

4 tablespoons white wine vinegar, divided

4 tablespoons unsalted butter

4 leeks, white and pale green parts only, thinly sliced

2 onions, diced

Sea salt

2 tablespoons polenta

4 cups fresh corn kernels, sliced from the cob, cobs reserved

2 quarts Basic Vegetable Broth (page 28)

1 fresh thyme sprig

1 cup heavy cream

½ tablespoon hot sauce

2 scallions, thinly sliced on a bias, for serving

1 In a glass jar, mix the jalapeños with 3 tablespoons of the vinegar and set aside.

2 In a large pot, melt the butter over medium-low heat. Cook the leeks and onions with a generous pinch of salt for 10 to 15 minutes until very soft.

3 Add the polenta, corn, corn cobs, broth, and thyme. Simmer for 30 minutes, until fragrant and slightly thick.

4 Add the heavy cream and simmer for another 15 minutes, until thick.

5 Remove the pot from the heat. Remove and discard the corn cobs and thyme.

6 Purée the soup with an immersion blender until smooth. For a very smooth soup, pass it through a china cap.

7 Stir in the remaining 1 tablespoon of vinegar and hot sauce. Season with salt.

8 Serve with the scallions and quick-pickled jalapeños.

9 Chill, cover, and store leftovers in the refrigerator for up to 2 days.

SUBSTITUTION TIP: Feel free to use olive oil in place of the butter and full-fat coconut milk in place of the heavy cream to make this soup vegan.

Nutritional Information Calories: 452; Saturated Fat: 14g; Carbohydrates: 57g; Sodium: 547mg; Fiber: 8g; Protein: 8g

CREAMY EDAMAME SOUP
WITH KALE & PICKLED ASPARAGUS

SERVES 4 TO 6 **PREP** 10 MINS **COOK** 5 MINS

■ GLUTEN-FREE ■ VEGAN

My college roommate was from Japan and introduced me to the beauty of edamame (soybeans) as a snack. It's a delicious vegan source of protein, without all of the processing that goes into many soy products. That's how edamame found its way into this creamy soup with kale and pickled asparagus.

1 bunch asparagus spears, tough ends discarded, spears and tips cut into 1½-inch pieces
¼ cup white wine vinegar
2 (16-ounce) packages frozen edamame
1 tablespoon soy sauce
Pinch wasabi powder
1 quart Basic Vegetable Broth (page 28)
1 tablespoon fresh lemon juice
2 to 4 kale leaves, shredded
Freshly ground black pepper

1 In a small nonreactive bowl, mix together the asparagus and vinegar. Transfer the bowl to the refrigerator.

2 Bring a large pot of water to a boil over high heat. Fill a large bowl with ice water and set it nearby. When the water begins to boil, add the edamame and blanch for 5 minutes, then immediately drain the edamame and transfer them to the ice water bath. Squeeze the edamame from their shells and discard the shells.

3 Place the shelled edamame in a blender along with the soy sauce, wasabi powder, vegetable broth, and lemon juice. Purée until smooth.

4 Pour the soup into individual serving bowls.

5 Drain the pickled asparagus and top each serving of soup with a few pieces and a small handful of shredded kale. Season with pepper.

COOKING TIP: To save time, purchase pre-shelled, blanched edamame. To make this gluten free, select gluten-free soy sauce.

Nutritional Information Calories: 365; Saturated Fat: 1g; Carbohydrates: 32g; Sodium: 402mg; Fiber: 10g; Protein: 30g

SOUP & COMFORT

BLACK BEAN SOUP

SERVES 4 TO 6 **PREP** 10 MINS **COOK** 25 MINS

■ GLUTEN-FREE ■ VEGAN ■ BIG 8 ALLERGEN–FRIENDLY

I like to soak and cook beans to improve their digestibility, but you can also use canned beans for convenience. Simply drain and rinse the beans before adding them to the soup. For extra protein, consider browning tempeh in a skillet over medium heat with oil and a pinch of chili powder. Use the cooked tempeh as a garnish for the finished soup.

1 teaspoon cumin seeds
1 tablespoon olive oil
1 onion, diced
6 garlic cloves, minced
1 celery stalk, diced
1 carrot, diced
¼ teaspoon red chili flakes
Sea salt
4 cups canned black beans
1 (15-ounce) can diced fire-
    roasted tomatoes
1 teaspoon smoked paprika
1 quart Roasted Vegetable Broth
    (page 29)
1 tablespoon red wine vinegar
Freshly ground black pepper
1 cup fresh cilantro leaves, for serving

1 In a large dry pot, toast the cumin seeds over medium heat until fragrant, about 1 to 2 minutes.

2 Carefully add the olive oil, onion, garlic, celery, carrot, and red chili flakes and a generous pinch of salt. Cook for 10 minutes.

3 Add the beans, tomatoes, paprika, and broth and cook for another 10 minutes. Stir in the red wine vinegar and season with pepper.

4 Remove 2 cups of the soup and purée in a blender until smooth. Return the purée to the soup pot. Adjust seasoning. Serve with fresh cilantro.

SUBSTITUTION TIP: If you don't observe a vegan diet, this soup is delicious with shredded sharp Cheddar and sour cream.

Nutritional Information Calories: 309; Saturated Fat: 1g; Carbohydrates: 49g; Sodium: 183mg; Fiber: 15g; Protein: 16g

FIRE-ROASTED VEGAN CHILI

SERVES 4 TO 6 **PREP** 15 MINS **COOK** 45 MINS

■ GLUTEN-FREE ■ VEGAN ■ BIG 8 ALLERGEN–FRIENDLY ■ FIX-AND-FORGET

This is the dish I come back to time and again for vegetarian comfort food, but it took me a while to find the exact recipe. The first time I tried to make vegetarian chili, I used a few cups of jalapeño peppers. If you like it hot, feel free to add a few to this chili.

2 tablespoons olive oil
2 onions, diced
4 celery stalks, diced
4 carrots, diced
2 cups thinly sliced mushrooms
4 bell peppers, thinly sliced
2 (15-ounce) cans diced fire-
    roasted tomatoes
2 (15-ounce) cans pinto beans, drained
    and rinsed
1 tablespoon smoked paprika
1 tablespoon ground cumin
1 teaspoon ground coriander
¼ teaspoon ground cinnamon
1 tablespoon ancho chili powder
Sea salt
Freshly ground black pepper
1 teaspoon freshly grated dark chocolate
1 cup fresh cilantro leaves, for serving

1 In a large pot, heat the olive oil and cook the onions, celery, and carrots over medium heat for 5 minutes, until slightly softened. Add the mushrooms and bell peppers and cook for another 5 minutes. Stir in the tomatoes, beans, paprika, cumin, coriander, cinnamon, and chili powder. Cover, season with salt and pepper, and cook for 30 minutes, until fragrant and stew-like.

2 Stir in the dark chocolate and adjust seasoning.

3 Serve with fresh cilantro.

COOKING TIP: Mix the paprika, cumin, coriander, cinnamon, and chili powder in a jar ahead of time so you're just a few steps from a hearty dinner.

Nutritional Information Calories: 529; Saturated Fat: 2g; Carbohydrates: 89g; Sodium: 676mg; Fiber: 29g; Protein: 26g

FIX-AND-FORGET: To make this soup in a slow cooker, simply place all of the ingredients in a 4-quart slow cooker and cook on low for 4 hours or on high for 2 hours.

RIBOLLITA ITALIAN BEAN
SOUP WITH MASCARPONE

SERVES 4 TO 6 **PREP** 10 MINS **COOK** 25 MINS

■ GLUTEN-FREE ■ VEGAN ■ VEGETARIAN

Ribollita is a classic Tuscan soup, but here it is transformed with mascarpone. This mild Italian soft cheese melts into the soup, infusing it with creaminess and providing a delicious contrast in texture, flavor, and temperature. Oh yeah, and the soup is pretty awesome, too!

2 tablespoons olive oil
1 onion, diced
2 carrots, diced
2 celery stalks, diced
2 garlic cloves, minced
¼ teaspoon red chili flakes
4 fresh thyme sprigs
1 quart Parmesan Broth (page 30)
1 (28-ounce) can whole peeled tomatoes, hand crushed
2 (15-ounce) cans cannellini beans, drained and rinsed, divided
1 bunch Lacinato kale, ribs removed, leaves thinly sliced
8 ounces mascarpone cheese, for serving

1 Heat the oil in a large pot over medium heat and cook the onion, carrots, celery, garlic, and red chili flakes for 5 minutes, until slightly softened.

2 Add the thyme, broth, and tomatoes, bring the liquid to a simmer, and cook for 15 minutes or until fragrant.

3 Remove the thyme sprigs and discard. Transfer 1 cup of the broth and vegetables to a blender along with 1 can of the cannellini beans. Purée until smooth.

4 Pour the puréed mixture back into the pot and bring the liquid back to a simmer.

5 Stir in the remaining can of beans and the kale and cook for 5 minutes, until the soup is thick and the kale is wilted.

6 To serve, ladle the soup into individual serving bowls and top each with a generous spoonful of mascarpone.

Nutritional Information Calories: 445; Saturated Fat: 6g; Carbohydrates: 58g; Sodium: 1129mg; Fiber: 16g; Protein: 22g

SOUP & COMFORT

VEGETARIAN POSOLE

SERVES 4 TO 6 **PREP** 10 MINS **COOK** 20 MINS

■ GLUTEN-FREE ■ VEGAN ■ BIG 8 ALLERGEN–FRIENDLY

Hominy is dried, hulled corn that has a tender-firm texture and serves as a base for posole (pronounced *poh-so-lay*). Like rice and noodles, it can take on a variety of flavors and toppings. So, let your imagination run wild and use this recipe as a base for experimentation.

1 bunch radishes, thinly sliced
¼ cup red wine vinegar
2 tablespoons olive oil
1 red onion, halved and thinly sliced
4 garlic cloves, minced
4 cups diced fresh tomatoes
2 quarts Basic Vegetable Broth (page 28)
1 teaspoon dried oregano
1 tablespoon ground cumin
1 teaspoon smoked paprika
2 (28-ounce) cans white hominy, drained
1 cup fresh cilantro leaves, for serving
4 limes, halved, for serving
8 to 12 corn tortillas, for serving

1 In a large bowl, toss the radishes with the vinegar and set in the refrigerator to marinate.

2 In a large pot, heat the olive oil over medium heat. Cook the onion, garlic, and tomatoes until soft and pulpy, about 10 minutes.

3 Add the broth, oregano, cumin, and paprika and bring to a simmer for 5 minutes. Add the hominy and cook for 5 more minutes to allow the flavors to come together.

4 Drain the radishes and set in a small bowl on a serving tray along with the cilantro, limes, and corn tortillas.

5 Ladle the soup into individual serving bowls and allow each person to garnish as desired.

6 Chill, cover, and store the leftover soup and toppings separately in the refrigerator for up to 4 days.

INGREDIENT TIP: Hominy is easy to find in the Mexican foods section of most grocery stores.

Nutritional Information Calories: 553; Saturated Fat: 2g; Carbohydrates: 102g; Sodium: 917mg; Fiber: 19g; Protein: 12g

VEGETARIAN SOUPS & STEWS

FRENCH ONION SOUP

SERVES 4 TO 6 **PREP** 10 MINS **COOK** 1 HOUR, 15 MINS

■ PALEO-FRIENDLY ■ GLUTEN-FREE ■ VEGETARIAN ■ BIG 8 ALLERGEN—FRIENDLY

For years I looked longingly at French onion soup, wishing I could make it for my husband, but I knew store-bought vegetable broths were no match for the beef broth called for in the recipe. Since he doesn't eat meat, I was out of luck. However, the Roasted Vegetable Broth (page 29) is so delicious, it is a perfect stand-in. Finally, a French onion soup everyone can enjoy!

2 tablespoons unsalted butter
2 tablespoons olive oil
6 onions, halved and thinly sliced
Sea salt
Pinch sugar
¼ cup dry red wine
2 quarts Roasted Vegetable Broth
  (page 29)

1 In a large pot, melt the butter with the olive oil over medium-low heat. Add the onions and season with a generous pinch of salt. Cover and cook for 30 minutes until the onions are very soft.

2 Remove the lid and add a pinch of sugar to the pan. Continue cooking for another 20 to 30 minutes, until the onions are golden brown.

3 Pour in the red wine and broth. Bring to a simmer and cook for 20 minutes allowing the flavors to come together.

4 Chill, cover, and store leftovers in the refrigerator for up to 3 days.

SUBSTITUTION TIP: For a Paleo and vegan soup, replace the butter with olive oil.

PAIRING TIP: This soup is delicious with Gourmet Grilled Cheese (page 217).

Nutritional Information Calories: 210; Saturated Fat: 5; Carbohydrates: 20g; Sodium: 247mg; Fiber: 4g; Protein: 2g

SOUP & COMFORT

182

BROCCOLI CHEESE SOUP

SERVES 4 TO 6 **PREP** 10 MINS **COOK** 20 MINS

■ GLUTEN-FREE ■ VEGETARIAN

When Rich and I first got married, we had a house fire and some of our friends took us in for a week. Looking back, I realize what an imposition we were! But our hosts were kind and generous and even worked hard to make vegetarian dishes for Rich, like this Broccoli Cheese Soup. The history of this recipe makes it another fine example of soup as a symbol of service, goodwill, and community.

1 broccoli head, broken into florets
2 garlic cloves, minced
2 quarts Basic Vegetable Broth (page 28)
1 cup heavy cream
16 ounces shredded Cheddar cheese
Sea salt
Freshly ground black pepper

1 In a large pot over medium heat, mix together the broccoli, garlic, and vegetable broth. Bring the liquid to a simmer, cover the pot, and cook until the broccoli is tender, about 15 minutes.

2 Stir in the heavy cream and cook for 5 minutes until thick. Remove the pot from the heat and stir in the shredded Cheddar until melted. Season with salt and pepper.

3 Chill, cover, and store leftovers in the refrigerator for up to 2 days.

PAIRING TIP: Serve this soup with 1 cup of Torn Baguette Croutons (page 197) per serving for a deliciously thick and chunky soup.

Nutritional Information Calories: 368; Saturated Fat: 12g; Carbohydrates: 17g; Sodium: 941mg; Fiber: 4g; Protein: 33g

VEGETARIAN SOUPS & STEWS

ZUCCHINI, CHICKPEA & LENTIL STEW

SERVES 4 TO 6 **PREP** 10 MINS **COOK** 20 MINS

■ GLUTEN-FREE ■ VEGAN ■ BIG 8 ALLERGEN–FRIENDLY

Vegetables are underestimated in both flavor and nutritional value. This stew is brimming with both. It makes a complete meal on its own, or it can be served with white or brown rice for a few more carbohydrates.

2 tablespoons olive oil
1 onion, diced
2 celery stalks, diced
2 garlic cloves, minced
½ teaspoon red chili flakes
1 zucchini, diced
1 roasted red bell pepper, diced
1 (15-ounce) can chickpeas, drained and rinsed
1 (15-ounce) can diced fire-roasted tomatoes, with juices
1 cup yellow or green lentils, rinsed and sorted
1 quart Basic Vegetable Broth (page 28)
1 tablespoon ancho chili powder
Sea salt
Freshly ground black pepper
Juice of 1 lemon
Fresh cilantro leaves, for serving
Lime wedges, for serving

1 In a large pot, heat the olive oil over medium heat. Cook the onion, celery, garlic, and red chili flakes for 5 minutes.

2 Add the zucchini and bell pepper and cook for 1 minute. Add the chickpeas, tomatoes, lentils, broth, and chili powder and bring to a simmer. Season generously with salt and pepper. Cover and cook for 20 minutes.

3 Stir in the lemon juice. Serve with fresh cilantro and lime wedges.

4 Chill, cover, and store leftovers in the refrigerator for up to 3 days.

INGREDIENT TIP: You can take this stew in many different directions. It works with Indian spices such as garam masala, turmeric, and ginger or Italian herbs such as rosemary, oregano, and basil.

Nutritional Information Calories: 439; Saturated Fat: 2g; Carbohydrates: 63g; Sodium: 251mg; Fiber: 24g; Protein: 24g

SAFFRON, GARLIC & POTATO SOUP

SERVES 4 TO 6 **PREP** 10 MINS **COOK** 35 MINS

■ GLUTEN-FREE ■ VEGAN ■ BIG 8 ALLERGEN–FRIENDLY

Rich went on a photography assignment for three weeks in India and offered to pick up some saffron for me. A street vendor told him it was expensive. "How much?" my husband asked. Turns out expense is relative because, for only $4, I've had a seemingly endless supply of saffron for the past three years.

1 onion, diced
6 garlic cloves, minced
2 pounds new potatoes, diced
2 quarts Basic Vegetable Broth (page 28)
Sea salt
Freshly ground black pepper
Pinch saffron
1 teaspoon white wine vinegar

1 In a large pot, mix together the onion, garlic, and potatoes. Cover with the broth and season generously with salt and pepper. Bring to a simmer over medium heat, cover the pot, and cook for 30 minutes, until the potatoes are soft.

2 Stir in the saffron and cook for 5 minutes to infuse the soup with flavor.

3 Stir in the vinegar.

4 Remove 2 cups of the soup and purée in a blender until smooth. Season with salt and pepper.

5 Chill, cover, and store leftovers in the refrigerator for up to 3 days.

INGREDIENT TIP: This soup has a subtle flavor that allows the saffron to shine, but if you're looking for other Indian flavors, add 1 teaspoon minced fresh ginger and ½ teaspoon ground turmeric. During the last 5 minutes of cooking, stir in ½ teaspoon garam masala.

Nutritional Information Calories: 195; Saturated Fat: 0g; Carbohydrates: 44g; Sodium: 214mg; Fiber: 7g; Protein: 5g

LENTIL SOUP

SERVES 4 TO 6 **PREP** 10 MINS **COOK** 1 HOUR, 15 MINS

■ GLUTEN-FREE ■ VEGAN ■ BIG 8 ALLERGEN—FRIENDLY

I love the holiday spices of this lentil soup, created by Rich's late Aunt Marilyn. She was a beautiful and kind woman who welcomed me and so many others into her home with open arms. The soup is especially delicious on the second day, after the flavors have had time to marry.

2 tablespoons olive oil
1 small onion, finely diced
2 carrots, finely diced
2 celery stalks, finely diced
2 garlic cloves, minced
½ cup diced green bell pepper
2 cups green lentils, rinsed and sorted
2 quarts Basic Vegetable Broth (page 28)
¼ cup tomato paste
⅛ teaspoon ground cloves
⅛ teaspoon allspice
Bouquet garni with 1 bay leaf, 3 thyme sprigs, and 3 parsley sprigs
2 cups peeled and diced potatoes
2 tablespoons red wine vinegar
Sea salt
Freshly ground black pepper
2 scallions, thinly sliced on a bias, for serving

1 In a large pot, heat the olive oil over medium heat. Cook the onion, carrots, celery, garlic, and bell pepper for 5 minutes.

2 Add the lentils, broth, tomato paste, cloves, allspice, and bouquet garni. Bring to a simmer, cover, and cook for 1 hour, until the lentils are very soft. Stir in the potatoes, cover, and cook for another 15 minutes until the potatoes are soft.

3 Stir in the red wine vinegar. Season with salt and pepper and adjust seasoning. Shower with scallions.

4 Chill, cover, and store leftovers in the refrigerator for up to 3 days.

COOKING TIP: This soup can easily be doubled to feed a crowd.

Nutritional Information Calories: 519; Saturated Fat: 1g; Carbohydrates: 83g; Sodium: 256mg; Fiber: 34g; Protein: 28g

VEGETARIAN SOUPS & STEWS

BLACK BEAN & SPINACH ENCHILADA SOUP

SERVES 4 TO 6 **PREP** 10 MINS **COOK** 20 MINS

■ GLUTEN-FREE ■ VEGETARIAN

This soup is perfect with loads of fresh tortilla chips and a cold beer or hard cider. The flavors are so enticing, no one will miss the meat, pleasing vegetarians and omnivores alike.

2 tablespoons olive oil
1 onion, diced
4 garlic cloves, minced
2 cans black beans, drained and rinsed
8 cups roughly chopped fresh spinach
2 (8-ounce) packages full-fat
    cream cheese
1 quart Basic Vegetable Broth (page 28)
1 tablespoon ground cumin
1 teaspoon smoked paprika
16 ounces shredded Cheddar cheese
1 cup store-bought enchilada sauce,
    for serving
Tortilla chips, for serving

1 In a large pot, heat the olive oil over medium heat. Cook the onion and garlic for 5 minutes. Add the black beans and cook for 1 minute. Stir in the spinach, and cook until just wilted.

2 Push the vegetables to the sides of the pot and place the cream cheese in the center. When the cream cheese has melted completely, after about 5 minutes, stir in the vegetable broth, cumin, and paprika. Bring the liquid to a simmer, then add the Cheddar cheese and stir until it is completely melted.

3 To serve, ladle the soup into individual serving bowls and drizzle the top with a few tablespoons of the enchilada sauce. Garnish with chips.

4 Chill, cover, and store leftovers in the refrigerator for up to 3 days.

INGREDIENT TIP: If you prefer to make your own enchilada sauce, mix 1 cup of tomato sauce with 1 tablespoon of onion powder, 1 teaspoon garlic powder, 1 tablespoon smoked paprika, and 1 teaspoon cayenne pepper.

Nutritional Information Calories: 1093; Saturated Fat: 50g; Carbohydrates: 37g; Sodium: 1181mg; Fiber: 11g; Protein: 48g

SOUP & COMFORT

DAL TADKA

SERVES 4 TO 6 **PREP** 10 MINS **COOK** 30 MINS

■ GLUTEN-FREE ■ VEGAN ■ BIG 8 ALLERGEN–FRIENDLY

Tadka is a culinary technique used in Indian cooking in which oil is infused with spices or herbs. The finished aromatic oil is then added to another dish to finish it or as a base for a curry. In this common dal recipe, tadka is added at the end of cooking.

1 cup yellow lentils
1 onion, diced
4 garlic cloves, minced
2 plum tomatoes, diced
1 teaspoon minced fresh ginger
1 teaspoon ground turmeric
½ teaspoon garam masala
3 cups Basic Vegetable Broth (page 28)
2 tablespoons canola oil
1 teaspoon cumin seeds
6 fresh curry leaves (optional)
2 dried red chiles
1 teaspoon black mustard seeds

1 In a large pot, mix together the lentils, onion, garlic, tomatoes, ginger, turmeric, garam masala, and vegetable broth. Bring to a simmer over medium heat, then reduce the heat to low, cover the pot, and cook for 30 minutes or until the lentils are very tender.

2 Meanwhile, in a small skillet, heat the canola oil over medium heat. Toast the cumin seeds for 1 minute, then add the curry leaves (if using), chili, and black mustard seeds. Cook for 30 seconds. Remove the skillet from the heat and allow the spices to infuse the oil.

3 When the lentils have finished cooking, spoon them into individual serving bowls. Drizzle each serving with some of the spiced oil.

4 Chill, cover, and store leftovers separately in the refrigerator for up to 3 days.

INGREDIENT TIP: You can find black mustard seeds and curry leaves at an Asian grocery store or online.

Nutritional Information Calories: 285; Saturated Fat: 1g; Carbohydrates: 40g; Sodium: 119mg; Fiber: 17g; Protein: 15g

MUSHROOM RISOTTO SOUP

SERVES 4 TO 6 **PREP** 10 MINS **COOK** 35 MINS

■ GLUTEN-FREE ■ VEGETARIAN

I worked in an Italian restaurant where we served risotto. Dinner guests who had never had the dish before were incredulous that it contained no cream. In risotto, the rice releases starch and thickens the broth as it is added. To make it into a creamy soup, simply continue adding broth after the rice has finished cooking.

2 quarts Roasted Vegetable Broth (page 29)
1 cup dried shiitake mushrooms
1 cup hot water
2 tablespoons olive oil
1 onion, diced
2 garlic cloves, minced
2 tablespoons unsalted butter
2 cups thinly sliced cremini mushrooms
2 cups Arborio or short-grain white rice
Sea salt
Freshly ground black pepper
½ cup dry white wine
1 tablespoon fresh thyme leaves

1 Place a large pot on the back burner of your stove and pour in the vegetable broth. Bring the broth to a simmer over medium-low heat.

2 Soak the mushrooms in the hot water until soft. Cut them into thin strips. Strain the soaking liquid into the simmering broth through a fine-mesh sieve lined with cheesecloth.

3 In a separate large pot, heat the olive oil over medium heat and cook the onion and garlic for 5 minutes. Push the vegetables to the sides of the pot, then melt the butter in the center of the pot and brown the mushrooms in batches, pushing them to the sides of the pot as you go.

4 Add the rice to the pot, season with salt and pepper, and stir to coat in the butter and oil.

5 Deglaze the pot with white wine, cooking for 2 to 3 minutes to evaporate the alcohol.

6 Add the thyme leaves and about 1 cup of the broth. Stir constantly with a wooden spoon until the rice absorbs all of the moisture.

7 Add another 1 or 2 cups of broth, stirring again until all moisture is absorbed. Season with salt and pepper as you go.

8 Continue adding broth and stirring until all of the moisture is absorbed. When the rice is tender but still slightly firm, add 2 more cups of broth and stir to integrate the flavors. Remove the pot from the heat, adjust the seasonings to taste, and serve.

9 Chill, cover, and refrigerate leftovers for up to 2 days.

COOKING TIP: For even more robust flavor, consider using the Parmesan Broth (page 30) and adding several thick shavings of Parmesan cheese to the soup.

Nutritional Information Calories: 542; Saturated Fat: 5g; Carbohydrates: 90g; Sodium: 338mg; Fiber: 5g; Protein: 9g

VEGETARIAN JAMBALAYA

SERVES 4 TO 6 **PREP** 10 MINS **COOK** 30 MINS

■ VEGETARIAN ■ VEGAN

I learned to make roux about the same time I learned to make jambalaya. Sure, I knew how to thicken soups and sauces with a basic butter and flour mixture, but to make a dark amber roux was a transformative experience. This soupy dish is perfect over rice or paired with simple crusty bread.

4 tablespoons unsalted butter

¼ cup all-purpose flour

2 tablespoons olive oil

1 onion, diced

2 carrots, diced

2 celery stalks, diced

1 yellow summer squash, diced

1 zucchini, diced

2 green bell peppers, cored and diced

1 red or yellow bell pepper, cored and diced

2 (15-ounce) cans diced fire-roasted tomatoes

1 quart Basic Vegetable Broth (page 28)

½ teaspoon allspice

1 tablespoon Worcestershire sauce

1 teaspoon minced fresh thyme

1 teaspoon dried marjoram

Sea salt

Freshly ground black pepper

½ cup fresh flat-leaf parsley leaves, for serving

2 lemons, cut into wedges, for serving

1 In a small skillet, melt the butter over medium-low heat until bubbling. Whisk in the flour and stir until a thick paste forms. Continue cooking for 15 to 20 minutes until dark brown and fragrant.

2 In a large pot, heat the olive oil over medium heat. Cook the onion, carrots, and celery for 5 minutes until slightly softened. Add the squash, zucchini, bell peppers, tomatoes, broth, allspice, Worcestershire sauce, thyme, and marjoram. Season generously with salt and pepper. Cook uncovered for 15 minutes, or until the vegetables are crisp tender.

3 Stir in the roux and cook until the jambalaya is just thickened.

4 Serve with fresh parsley and lemon wedges.

5 Chill, cover, and store leftovers in the refrigerator for up to 2 days.

SUBSTITUTION TIP: For a vegan jambalaya, you can use canola oil in place of the butter. The aroma will not be quite as strong, but it will work to thicken the stew just as well.

Nutritional Information Calories: 333; Saturated Fat: 9g; Carbohydrates: 37g; Sodium: 376mg; Fiber: 9g; Protein: 7g

9

SALADS, SANDWICHES
& SOUP TOPPINGS

Croutons Three Ways 196

Torn Baguette Croutons 197

Paleo Sage Breadsticks 198

Fresh Tomato & Mint Salad 199

Kale Salad with Spicy
Lemon Vinaigrette 200

Savoy Cabbage & Apple Slaw 201

Frisée with Red & Yellow Peppers,
Cucumber & Goat Cheese 202

Tangled Vegetable Noodle Salad
with Miso Dressing 205

Lentil Salad with Cherries & Basil 207

Cold Rice Noodle Salad with
Sesame Vinaigrette 208

Grilled Chicken Salad with Pickled
Currants & Toasted Hazelnuts 210

Roasted Vegetable & Quinoa
Salad with Pepitas 212

Kale Salad with Pomegranate & Orange
Basil Vinaigrette 215

Egg Salad with Basil & Paprika 216

Gourmet Grilled Cheese 217

Caprese Panini 218

Crab, Mint & Corn Grilled Cheese 219

Roasted Red Pepper & Halloumi
Sandwich with Hummus 220

Smoked Trout with Arugula &
Creamy Dill Sauce on Rye 221

Banh Mi 222

CROUTONS THREE WAYS

YIELDS 4 CUPS **PREP** 5 MINS **COOK** 15 MINS

■ GLUTEN-FREE ■ VEGAN

Croutons add an extra layer of texture and flavor to soups and salads. Making your own at home allows you to control all of the ingredients to customize the flavors and adapt the recipe to your dietary restrictions. This recipe works equally well with gluten-free breads, sourdough, whole-wheat, or even Paleo quick breads. The basic recipe involves bread cubes, olive oil, salt, and pepper. I have also included three distinct flavoring options you can use if you wish—fresh herbs, grated Parmesan, and dried mushroom powder.

4 cups cubed bread
¼ cup olive oil
Sea salt
Freshly ground black pepper
1 tablespoon chopped fresh herbs, such as parsley, thyme, rosemary, or oregano (optional)
¼ cup grated Parmesan (optional)
1 tablespoon dried mushroom powder (optional)

1 Preheat the oven to 400°F.

2 Line a sheet pan with parchment paper.

3 In a large bowl, toss the cubed bread with the olive oil and season generously with salt and pepper. Toss in the herbs, Parmesan, and dried mushroom powder (if using).

4 Spread the coated bread out on the sheet pan and transfer the sheet pan to the oven.

5 Roast uncovered for 15 minutes until the croutons are lightly browned. Remove the baking sheet from the oven and let the croutons cool completely.

6 Use immediately or store in an airtight container at room temperature for up to 3 days.

INGREDIENT TIP: To make dried mushroom powder, place about ¼ cup of dried shiitake mushrooms in a spice grinder and pulse until finely ground. To make this Paleo, use a Paleo-friendly bread made with eggs and nut flour.

Nutritional Information (½ cup) Calories: 78; Saturated Fat: 1g; Carbohydrates: 2g; Sodium: 95mg; Fiber: 1g; Protein: 2g

TORN BAGUETTE CROUTONS

YIELDS 8 CUPS   **PREP** 5 MINS   **COOK** 15 MINS

■ VEGETARIAN

The texture of torn croutons is a nice change of pace from the traditional cubes. I love how the bread gets crispy on the outside but stays tender and chewy on the inside. The croutons can also be made with gluten-free bread, but they're best if the bread has not yet been sliced. These are delicious in puréed soups and on Grilled Chicken Salad with Pickled Currants & Toasted Hazelnuts (page 210).

1 French baguette
¼ cup olive oil
2 tablespoons melted unsalted butter
Sea salt
Freshly ground black pepper

1 Preheat the oven to 400°F. Line a sheet pan with parchment paper.

2 Hand tear the baguette into 1- to 2-inch pieces, including crusts.

3 In a large mixing bowl, whisk the olive oil and melted butter together and swirl it so that it coats the sides of the bowl. Place the torn bread pieces in the bowl and toss gently to lightly coat all of the pieces.

4 Spread them across the sheet pan and season with salt and pepper.

5 Bake for 15 minutes until lightly browned, turning once.

6 Allow to cool completely before storing in an airtight container for up to 3 days.

PREPARATION TIP: For a slightly more refined crouton with a smoother texture, remove the crusts from the bread before tearing into individual pieces.

Nutritional Information (½ cup) Calories: 109; Saturated Fat: 2g; Carbohydrates: 14g; Sodium: 182mg; Fiber: 1g; Protein: 3g

PALEO SAGE BREADSTICKS

SERVES 4 TO 6 **PREP** 15 MINS **COOK** 13 TO 14 MINS

■ PALEO ■ GLUTEN-FREE ■ VEGETARIAN

My kids and I cannot eat wheat, so fresh breadsticks are a distant memory. But one evening I needed an accompaniment to our soup dinner and decided to use almond meal and a mix of gluten-free flours. They were so easy to whip up, I invited the kids into the kitchen to help me shape them into long shapes. My youngest son was so proud of himself, he bragged at dinner, "I helped roll these out, Daddy!" They were such a delicious surprise! Be brave and experiment with substitutions.

¾ cup blanched almond flour
¼ cup arrowroot powder
¼ cup tapioca flour
¼ teaspoon sea salt
¼ teaspoon baking soda
1 egg
1 tablespoon olive oil
1 teaspoon maple syrup
1 tablespoon minced fresh sage

1 Preheat the oven to 350°F. Line a sheet pan with parchment paper.

2 In a small mixing bowl, mix the almond flour, arrowroot, tapioca flour, sea salt, and baking soda. Whisk in the egg, olive oil, maple syrup, and sage and stir until mixed thoroughly.

3 Form the mixture into 6 small balls and roll out with the heel of your hand into long spears.

4 Carefully transfer them to the pan and bake for 13 to 14 minutes, until just beginning to brown.

5 Cool completely before storing in an airtight container for up to 2 days.

SUBSTITUTION TIP: To make garlic bread sticks, replace the sage with ½ teaspoon of garlic powder and sprinkle ¼ teaspoon of garlic salt over the top of the breadsticks just before baking.

Nutritional Information Calories: 230; Saturated Fat: 2g; Carbohydrates: 18g; Sodium: 223mg; Fiber: 3g; Protein: 6g

FRESH TOMATO & MINT SALAD

SERVES 4 TO 6 **PREP** 5 MINS **COOK** 0 MINS

■ PALEO ■ GLUTEN-FREE ■ VEGAN ■ BIG 8 ALLERGEN—FRIENDLY

In my mind, the community garden in our neighborhood is a cross between the Garden of Eden and Jurassic Park. Squash plants pour over the bounds of each garden plot and sunflowers tower over cornstalks. Bees and butterflies fill the space with a faint hum. At the end of August, the garden is teeming with life . . . and tomatoes! Lots of them. So many that we simply could not pick them all. Sometimes tomatoes are added to a green salad, but when they're in season, they should take center stage.

2 pounds fresh heirloom tomatoes, larger ones halved or thinly sliced
2 shallots, halved and cut into thin slices
1 cup fresh mint leaves, roughly chopped
¼ cup olive oil
2 tablespoons red wine vinegar
Sea salt
Freshly ground black pepper

1 In a large serving bowl, mix the tomatoes, shallots, and mint.

2 Drizzle with the olive oil and vinegar, season with salt and pepper, and give everything a gentle toss.

3 Allow to sit for at least 30 minutes to allow the flavors to mix thoroughly. This salad is best enjoyed immediately.

INGREDIENT TIP: For the best flavor, grow your own tomatoes or purchase them from a farmers' market. Tomatoes at the grocery store, even the "vine-ripened" ones, are bred for transportation, not flavor.

Nutritional Information Calories: 203; Saturated Fat: 2g; Carbohydrates: 19g; Sodium: 66mg; Fiber: 6g; Protein: 5g

KALE SALAD
WITH SPICY LEMON VINAIGRETTE

SERVES 4 TO 6 **PREP** 10 MINS **COOK** 0 MINS

■ PALEO ■ GLUTEN-FREE ■ VEGAN ■ BIG 8 ALLERGEN–FRIENDLY

Kale has ridden the wave of popularity and found its way into smoothies, chips, and even chocolate. These days, raw kale seems almost passé. But when I first tasted this salad, I knew it would be with me for life. It's my go-to recipe anytime I have kale in the house. Even the kids are learning to like it! You can use whatever variety of kale you like: Lacinato, green, or red.

1 bunch kale, ribs removed
Zest and juice of 1 lemon
2 garlic cloves, minced
1 teaspoon red wine vinegar
¼ teaspoon red chili flakes
¼ cup olive oil
Sea salt

1 Roughly chop the kale leaves and set aside.

2 In a large salad bowl, whisk together the lemon zest and juice, garlic, vinegar, red chili flakes, and olive oil. Season with salt.

3 Add the chopped kale to the salad bowl and use your hands to coat it in the dressing. Serve immediately.

4 The undressed greens and dressing can be stored separately in covered containers in the refrigerator until ready to serve. The dressing can be stored for up to 4 days.

COOKING TIP: To make this salad an entrée, add cooked chicken, diced avocado, and grated Parmesan. For a vegan entrée salad, add roasted vegetables and hemp hearts.

Nutritional Information Calories: 160; Saturated Fat: 2g; Carbohydrates: 11g; Sodium: 103mg; Fiber: 2g; Protein: 3g

SAVOY CABBAGE & APPLE SLAW

SERVES 4 TO 6 **PREP** 10 MINS **COOK** 0 MINS

■ PALEO ■ GLUTEN-FREE ■ VEGAN ■ BIG 8 ALLERGEN–FRIENDLY

We had another married couple over for dinner one evening. When I served this salad, the husband couldn't get over how delicious and unexpected the flavors were and caught himself as he compared it to the food they usually ate at home. We all laughed as his wife told him he was on thin ice. So, if you're used to the usual flavor of coleslaw, prepare to be amazed!

1 head savoy cabbage, shredded
2 Granny Smith apples, cored
  and julienned
1 red onion, halved and then thinly sliced
½ cup mayonnaise
Zest and juice of 1 lemon
1 tablespoon ground cumin
½ teaspoon smoked paprika
Pinch sugar
Sea salt
Freshly ground black pepper

1 In a large mixing bowl, toss together the cabbage, apples, and red onion.

2 In a medium bowl, whisk together the mayonnaise, lemon zest and juice, cumin, paprika, and sugar. Season with salt and pepper.

3 Just before serving, drizzle the dressing over the salad and stir to mix thoroughly. Enjoy the same day.

PREPARATION TIP: Feel free to prepare all of the ingredients ahead of time. Sprinkle the apple pieces with lemon juice and keep the onion in a separate container. Wait to toss the salad with the dressing until just prior to serving. To keep this allergen-free and vegan, use a vegan mayonnaise without soybean oil.

Nutritional Information Calories: 224; Saturated Fat: 2g; Carbohydrates: 33g; Sodium: 304mg; Fiber: 8g; Protein: 3g

FRISÉE
WITH RED & YELLOW PEPPERS, CUCUMBER & GOAT CHEESE

SERVES 4 TO 6 **PREP** 10 MINS **COOK** 0 MINS

▪ PALEO ▪ GLUTEN-FREE ▪ VEGETARIAN ▪ BIG 8 ALLERGEN–FRIENDLY

I just adore the lacy texture and appearance of frisée. It is naturally bitter and pairs well with baby spinach, sweet red and yellow bell peppers, spicy radishes, and tangy goat cheese all bathed in a honey-champagne vinaigrette. By feasting first with your eyes, you get to enjoy this meal twice.

FOR THE DRESSING

Juice of 1 lemon
¼ cup champagne vinegar
1 garlic clove, minced
1 tablespoon honey
½ teaspoon Dijon mustard
1 teaspoon minced fresh tarragon
½ cup olive oil
Sea salt
Freshly ground black pepper

FOR THE SALAD

2 heads frisée, roughly torn
4 cups packed baby spinach
1 red bell pepper, cored and thinly sliced
1 yellow bell pepper, cored and thinly sliced
1 cucumber, sliced in long "noodles" with a vegetable peeler
3 to 4 radishes, thinly sliced
6 ounces goat cheese, crumbled into bite-size pieces

continued

FRISÉE WITH RED & YELLOW PEPPERS, CUCUMBER & GOAT CHEESE *continued*

TO MAKE THE DRESSING

1 In a medium bowl, whisk together the lemon juice, vinegar, garlic, honey, mustard, and tarragon.

2 Slowly drizzle in the olive oil, whisking constantly to emulsify.

3 Season with salt and pepper.

TO MAKE THE SALAD

1 In a large mixing bowl, toss together the frisée, spinach, bell peppers, cucumber, and radishes.

2 Drizzle the dressing over the salad and mix gently with your hands.

3 Divide the salad among individual serving dishes and top with goat cheese.

4 Store the salad and dressing separately in the refrigerator for up to 2 days.

INGREDIENT TIP: Many people who are allergic to cow milk find they can enjoy goat milk. Although the flavor is quite assertive the first time you try it, goat cheese is quite delectable and has become one of my favorite soft cheeses.

Nutritional Information Calories: 487; Saturated Fat: 14g; Carbohydrates: 18g; Sodium: 284mg; Fiber: 6g; Protein: 17g

TANGLED VEGETABLE NOODLE SALAD
WITH MISO DRESSING

SERVES 4 TO 6 **PREP** 15 MINS **COOK** 0 MINS

■ PALEO-FRIENDLY ■ GLUTEN-FREE ■ VEGAN ■ BIG 8 ALLERGEN–FRIENDLY

For a while I became very interested in the raw food movement. I loved the bright, beautiful flavors of raw foods and the effortless preparation and cleanup. Want a snack? It's ready in about 5 minutes. No defrosting. No cooking. No waiting. This was and still is my favorite energy-loaded vegan lunch to take to the beach.

FOR THE DRESSING

¼ cup white miso
2 tablespoons olive oil
1½ tablespoons sesame oil
1 tablespoon soy sauce
1 tablespoon grated fresh ginger
Freshly ground black pepper

FOR THE SALAD

2 beets, peeled
4 carrots, scrubbed
6 cups spring mix
1 cup roughly chopped fresh cilantro
2 scallions, thinly sliced on a bias
½ cup roughly chopped roasted almonds

TO MAKE THE DRESSING

1 In a small bowl, whisk together the miso, olive and sesame oils, soy sauce, and ginger.

2 Season with freshly ground pepper.

TO MAKE THE SALAD

1 With a vegetable spiralizer, make spiral noodles with the beets and carrots. If you do not have a spiralizer, use a vegetable peeler to make long, thin noodles.

2 In a large mixing bowl, mix the vegetable noodles with the spring mix, cilantro, and scallions and toss with the miso dressing.

continued

TANGLED VEGETABLE NOODLE SALAD
WITH MISO DRESSING *continued*

3 Divide the salad among individual serving dishes and top with the roasted almonds.

4 The salad ingredients and dressing can be in separate covered containers in the refrigerator for 1 to 2 days until ready to serve.

SUBSTITUTION TIP: To make this Paleo and soy-free, swap the miso for 1 teaspoon of hot Chinese mustard, double the sesame oil, and replace the soy sauce with coconut aminos. For nut allergies, leave out the roasted almonds. To make it wheat- and gluten-free, use gluten-free soy sauce.

NUTRITIONAL INFORMATION CALORIES: 275; Saturated Fat: 2g; Carbohydrates: 22g; Sodium: 996mg; Fiber: 6g; Protein: 7g

LENTIL SALAD
WITH CHERRIES & BASIL

SERVES 4 TO 6 **PREP** 10 MINS **COOK** 20 MINS

■ GLUTEN-FREE ■ VEGAN ■ BIG 8 ALLERGEN–FRIENDLY

When my second son was born, a long lost friend sent me a message saying she had seen my picture in *Pregnancy and Newborn* magazine. She took it as a sign that we should reconnect and invited our family over for dinner in late August. I wanted to find a recipe that was simple enough to throw together at the last minute but bursting with the flavors of the season. This cold lentil salad was easy to prepare ahead of time and store in the refrigerator until just before serving, though the cherries and basil are best added at the last minute.

2 cups dried lentils, rinsed and sorted
5 cups water
Sea salt
2 cups fresh black cherries, pitted
    and halved
2 scallions, thinly sliced on a bias
1 cup fresh basil leaves, roughly chopped
¼ cup red wine vinegar
2 tablespoons olive oil
Freshly ground black pepper

1 Bring the water to a simmer in a large pot over medium heat. Add the lentils and a generous pinch of salt and cook them for 20 minutes or until they are tender but not falling apart. Drain the lentils and transfer them to a large bowl. Cover and store in the refrigerator until completely chilled.

2 Just before serving, add the cherries, scallions, and basil to the chilled lentils and toss well.

3 In a small bowl, whisk the red wine vinegar and olive oil together and season with salt and pepper. Pour over the salad and toss gently to mix thoroughly.

4 The salad is best enjoyed immediately, but leftovers may be stored for 1 day in the refrigerator.

COOKING TIP: For extra flavor, cook the lentils in Basic Vegetable Broth (page 28).

Nutritional Information Calories: 443; Saturated Fat: 1g; Carbohydrates: 68g; Sodium: 66mg; Fiber: 31g; Protein: 26g

COLD RICE NOODLE SALAD
WITH SESAME VINAIGRETTE

SERVES 4 TO 6 **PREP** 15 MINS **COOK** 0 MINS

■ GLUTEN-FREE ■ VEGAN ■ BIG 8 ALLERGEN–FRIENDLY

The dressing on this salad is so good I could drink it. Together with the greens, herbs, and vegetables, it has the perfect balance of salty, sour, sweet, spicy, and crunchy. If you've never tried fresh mint in your salad, you're in for a treat.

FOR THE DRESSING

¼ cup rice vinegar
Zest and juice of 2 limes
1 tablespoon packed brown sugar
¼ teaspoon red chili flakes
1 tablespoon soy sauce
1 tablespoon toasted sesame oil
½ cup canola oil
Sea salt
Freshly ground black pepper

FOR THE SALAD

8 ounces rice vermicelli noodles
8 cups spring mix
1 cup fresh basil leaves, hand torn
1 cup roughly chopped fresh cilantro
½ cup fresh mint leaves
1 cucumber, diced
1 cup roughly chopped peanuts

TO MAKE THE DRESSING

1 In a small bowl, whisk together the vinegar, lime zest and juice, brown sugar, red chili flakes, and soy sauce.

2 Slowly drizzle in the sesame oil and canola oil, whisking constantly to emulsify.

3 Season with salt and pepper.

TO MAKE THE SALAD

1 Soak the rice noodles in warm water for 15 minutes or until soft. Drain and set in a large serving dish.

2 Pour half of the dressing over the rice noodles.

3 In a separate bowl, mix the spring mix, basil, cilantro, mint, and cucumber. Toss with the remaining dressing and then place atop the noodles. Shower the whole thing with the chopped peanuts and serve immediately.

4 The salad ingredients and dressing can be stored separately in a covered container in the refrigerator for 1 to 2 days until ready to serve.

COOKING TIP: To accommodate for peanut allergies, replace the peanuts with roasted almonds or omit them all together. To make it wheat- and gluten-free, use gluten-free soy sauce. To make it soy-free, use coconut aminos instead of soy sauce.

Nutritional Information Calories: 744; Saturated Fat: 5g; Carbohydrates: 61g; Sodium: 539mg; Fiber: 6g; Protein: 16g

GRILLED CHICKEN SALAD
WITH PICKLED CURRANTS & TOASTED HAZELNUTS

SERVES 4 TO 6 **PREP** 15 MINS **COOK** 15 MINS

▪ PALEO ▪ GLUTEN-FREE ▪ BIG 8 ALLERGEN–FRIENDLY

When I moved to Los Angeles, one of the first restaurants I tried was a trendy, family-friendly joint with wood-fired pizza, a rooftop garden, and a live DJ who spun hipster music oblivious to the hordes of children scurrying over cement floors. Of course, they even had gluten-free pizza crusts. They also had deliciously unpredictable salads. This is my take on their grilled chicken salad, and I just have to say, pickled currants are a revelation!

½ cup currants
¼ cup red wine vinegar
¼ cup plus 2 tablespoons olive oil, divided
4 to 6 boneless, skinless chicken breasts, pounded to a uniform ¾-inch thickness
Sea salt
Freshly ground black pepper
4 heads little gem or butter lettuce
2 heads radicchio
1 shallot, minced
2 cups Torn Baguette Croutons (page 197), for serving
½ cup hazelnuts, toasted and roughly chopped, for serving

1 In a jar, mix the currants and red wine vinegar and set aside. You can do this a day in advance if you wish.

2 Heat a grill pan over medium heat or preheat your outdoor grill.

3 If using a pan, brush it with 2 tablespoons of the olive oil. If using an outdoor grill, preheat the grates over medium heat before brushing with oil.

4 Season the chicken breasts with salt and pepper. Sear on each side for 5 to 7 minutes, or until cooked through and the juices run clear. Set on a cutting board to rest.

5 Hand tear the lettuce into a large mixing bowl. Use a sharp chef's knife to thinly slice the radicchio and add it to the bowl.

6 Strain the currants, reserving the vinegar to make the dressing, and add to the salad.

7 In a small bowl, whisk the vinegar together with the remaining ¼ cup of olive oil and shallot. Season with salt and pepper.

8 Pour the dressing over the salad and toss to mix thoroughly.

9 Slice each chicken breast into several pieces and add to the salad.

10 Divide the salad among individual serving plates. Top with the croutons and toasted hazelnuts.

11 Serve immediately.

12 If you wish to prepare this in advance, store the dressing, salad, croutons, nuts, and chicken separately in the refrigerator. The dressing will keep for up to 5 days.

INGREDIENT TIP: Many firm vegetables and fruits take on a delightfully surprising flavor when quick-pickled. Let your imagination run wild and pickle blanched green beans, fresh plums, beets, or whatever is in season.

Nutritional Information Calories: 673; Saturated Fat: 7g; Carbohydrates: 26g; Sodium: 333mg; Fiber: 5g; Protein: 54g

ROASTED VEGETABLE & QUINOA SALAD
WITH PEPITAS

SERVES 4 TO 6 **PREP** 15 MINS **COOK** 40 MINS

■ GLUTEN-FREE ■ VEGAN ■ BIG 8 ALLERGEN—FRIENDLY

I love vegetables, especially when they're roasted until browned and caramelized. This salad is an awesome vegan entrée on its own, but it can also be served with a simple puréed soup, such as Curried Sweet Potato Soup (page 62) or Cream of Mushroom Soup (page 69). You can serve it hot or chilled and take it with you for a savory picnic lunch.

2 beets, peeled and quartered
4 carrots, cut into 2-inch pieces
2 zucchini, cut into 1-inch pieces
4 shallots, quartered
1 pint grape tomatoes
½ cup olive oil, divided
1 tablespoon fresh thyme leaves
Sea salt
Freshly ground black pepper
2 cups quinoa
1 quart Basic Vegetable Broth (page 28) or water
¼ cup red wine vinegar
6 cups spring mix
½ cup pepitas, for serving

1 Preheat the oven to 375°F.

2 In a large bowl, toss the beets, carrots, zucchini, shallots, and tomatoes with ¼ cup of olive oil and thyme. Spread the mixture out on a baking sheet and season with salt and pepper. Roast the vegetables for 35 to 40 minutes or until they are browned and slightly caramelized.

3 Bring the vegetable broth to a simmer in a large pot over medium heat, and add the quinoa. Reduce the heat to low, cover the pot, and cook for about 20 minutes or until the quinoa absorbs all of the water. Fluff with a fork.

4 In a small bowl, whisk together the remaining ¼ cup of olive oil with the red wine vinegar. Season with salt and pepper.

5 Just before you're ready to serve, toss the spring mix and roasted vegetables with the dressing and serve over the quinoa. Top with pepitas.

6 Store leftover vegetables, quinoa, spring mix, and dressing separately for up to 3 days.

VARIATION TIP: This salad is also delicious with wild rice instead of quinoa.

Nutritional Information Calories: 667; Saturated Fat: 5g; Carbohydrates: 77g; Sodium: 207mg; Fiber: 12g; Protein: 18g

KALE SALAD
WITH POMEGRANATE & ORANGE BASIL VINAIGRETTE

SERVES 4 TO 6 **PREP** 10 MINS **COOK** 0 MINS

■ PALEO-FRIENDLY ■ GLUTEN-FREE ■ VEGAN ■ BIG 8 ALLERGEN–FRIENDLY

Although we came to California over two years ago, I am still smitten with this place, especially the way food just grows everywhere! We had a pomegranate tree growing outside our kitchen window in Los Angeles, and I plucked every piece of fruit I could reach. The fruit is in season in November and December, so serve this delicious salad with your holiday meal.

FOR THE DRESSING

Zest and juice of 1 orange
¼ cup balsamic vinegar
½ cup olive oil
Sea salt
Freshly ground black pepper

FOR THE SALAD

2 bunches kale, ribs removed, leaves roughly chopped
1 red onion, halved and sliced thinly
Arils from 1 pomegranate
1 carrot, shredded
4 ounces Gorgonzola cheese, crumbled

TO MAKE THE DRESSING

1 In a medium bowl, whisk together the orange zest and juice and balsamic vinegar.

2 Slowly drizzle in the olive oil, whisking constantly to emulsify.

3 Season with salt and pepper.

TO MAKE THE SALAD

1 In a large mixing bowl, toss together the kale, onion, pomegranate, and carrot.

2 Pour the dressing over the salad and toss gently to mix thoroughly.

3 Divide the salad among individual serving plates and top with crumbled Gorgonzola.

SUBSTITUTION TIP: For a vegan and allergen-free version, replace the cheese with cooled cooked new potatoes, radishes, and carrots. To make it Paleo, swap the Gorgonzola with nut cheese or leave it out.

Nutritional Information Calories: 425; Saturated Fat: 9g; Carbohydrates: 27g; Sodium: 483mg; Fiber: 4g; Protein: 11g

EGG SALAD WITH BASIL & PAPRIKA

SERVES 4 **PREP** 10 MINS **COOK** 0 MINS

■ PALEO ■ GLUTEN-FREE ■ VEGETARIAN

I'm so glad that egg yolks have finally been exonerated and their virtues extolled—they're loaded with essential nutrients, and they are a great vegetarian source of protein. If you keep hard-boiled eggs on hand, this salad is easy to whip up and is just as good on bread as it is on top of a big bowl of salad greens.

8 eggs
1 tablespoon Dijon mustard
¼ cup mayonnaise
8 slices bread or 8 cups salad greens
½ teaspoon smoked paprika
12 fresh basil leaves
Freshly ground black pepper

SUBSTITUTION TIP: To make this Paleo, simply omit the bread and serve this delicious salad on a bed of lettuce. Also, use a homemade or store-bought Paleo-friendly mayonnaise.

Nutritional Information (with bread) Calories: 235; Saturated Fat: 4g; Carbohydrates: 14g; Sodium: 395mg; Fiber: 1g; Protein: 13g

1 Place the eggs in a large pot and fill the pot with cold water. Bring the water to a boil over medium heat, then cover the pot, remove it from the stove, and set a timer for 15 minutes.

2 Meanwhile, fill a large bowl with ice water. When the timer goes off, immediately drain the water from the pot and plunge the cooked eggs into the ice water to halt the cooking process. This also prevents the yolks from developing a gray hue between the whites.

3 Peel the eggs carefully under running water, then chop them roughly into small and large dice.

4 Transfer the chopped eggs to a small bowl along with the mustard and mayonnaise and mix well.

5 Spread the mixture on slices of bread or scoop a few spoonfuls over salad greens.

6 Sprinkle with smoked paprika and garnish with basil. Season generously with pepper.

216

GOURMET GRILLED CHEESE

SERVES 4 **PREP** 10 MINS **COOK** 10 MINS

■ GLUTEN-FREE ■ VEGETARIAN

Sure, you could make a fine grilled cheese sandwich with Cheddar on white bread. It's a classic. But this grown-up grilled cheese has all of the delicious elements of the original—crisp toasted bread and melty cheese—with more complex flavors and more interesting textures. Whatever you do, make sure to dunk it into a bowl of Creamy Tomato Soup (page 63).

8 slices French boule, ciabatta, or gluten-free bread
½ cup (1 stick) unsalted butter, at room temperature
8 ounces Fontina cheese, sliced
8 ounce Parmigiano-Reggiano, sliced

1 Butter each slice of bread on *both* sides with ½ tablespoon of room temperature butter.

2 Divide the cheeses among half the buttered bread slices and then top with the remaining bread slices to make a sandwich.

3 Heat a large skillet over medium heat until hot. Place the sandwiches in the skillet and cook for 4 minutes until golden brown. Flip carefully and repeat on the opposite side.

4 Allow to rest for a few minutes, then slice and serve.

PAIRING TIP: For cheesy croutons to float in your soup, use the ingredients above and toast the buttered bread slices under a broiler, turn over, and top with the cheese. Slide back under the broiler until the cheese is browned and bubbling. They are amazing with the French Onion Soup (page 182).

Nutritional Information Calories: 654; Saturated Fat: 34g; Carbohydrates: 12g; Sodium: 1266mg; Fiber: 0g; Protein: 34g

SALADS, SANDWICHES & SOUP TOPPINGS

CAPRESE PANINI

SERVES 4 **PREP** 5 MINS **COOK** 10 MINS

■ GLUTEN-FREE ■ VEGETARIAN

Technically, without a panini press, this is nothing more than a glorified grilled cheese. But I promise, it will taste just as good as the real thing! Make sure to use fresh basil and vine-ripened tomatoes. I prefer beefsteak heirloom tomatoes.

¼ cup olive oil
2 large tomatoes
4 fresh basil leaves, roughly chopped
2 (4-ounce) balls fresh mozzarella, sliced
8 slices bread
¼ cup balsamic vinegar reduction

1 In a large skillet, heat the oil over medium heat.

2 Divide the tomatoes, basil, and mozzarella among 4 slices of the bread. Drizzle with 1 tablespoon of balsamic reduction and top with a second slice of bread to make a sandwich.

3 Carefully transfer each of the sandwiches to the skillet and cook for about 4 minutes on each side until golden brown. Press down on the top slice of bread with a spatula. Flip carefully and repeat on the opposite side, again pressing down with the spatula.

4 Serve immediately.

SUBSTITUTION TIP: To make this gluten-free, use gluten-free bread.

INGREDIENT TIP: You can find balsamic reduction at a specialty market or make your own by cooking 1 cup of balsamic vinegar over low heat until it is reduced to ¼ cup, about 15 minutes. Be careful to keep it just below a simmer so as not to scorch it.

Nutritional Information Calories: 314; Saturated Fat: 8g; Carbohydrates: 15g; Sodium: 297mg; Fiber: 2g; Protein: 12g;

SOUP & COMFORT

CRAB, MINT & CORN GRILLED CHEESE

SERVES 4 **PREP** 5 MINS **COOK** 10 MINS

■ GLUTEN-FREE

Every Labor Day, my family visited the San Juan Islands off the coast of northern Washington. We would catch crab all day and then spend the evening on the beach cooking it with corn on the cob in a large metal drum. All we needed was a crock of clarified butter and life was perfect. It's been over a decade since I've gone up to the Islands, but crab and corn still take me right back. Mint and grilled cheese are comforting embellishments.

4 tablespoons unsalted butter, at room temperature
8 slices wheat bread or gluten-free bread
½ cup fresh corn kernels
¼ cup roughly chopped fresh mint
16 ounces lump crabmeat
Sea salt
Freshly ground black pepper
8 ounce fontina cheese, sliced

1 Spread the butter on one side of all of the bread slices.

2 In a small mixing bowl, mix the corn, mint, and crabmeat. Season with salt and pepper.

3 Divide the mixture among 4 of the slices of bread. Top with the fontina cheese and then top with the remaining slice to make a sandwich.

4 Carefully transfer each of the sandwiches to the skillet and cook for about 4 minutes on each side until golden brown. Press down on the top slice of bread with a spatula. Flip carefully and repeat on the opposite side, again pressing down with the spatula.

5 Serve immediately.

COOKING TIP: Make sure to pick over the crabmeat to check for shells before adding it to the sandwich filling.

Nutritional Information Calories: 561; Saturated Fat: 19g; Carbohydrates: 30g; Sodium: 1500mg; Fiber: 5g; Protein: 39g

ROASTED RED PEPPER & HALLOUMI SANDWICH
WITH HUMMUS

SERVES 4 TO 6 **PREP** 10 MINS **COOK** 8 MINS

■ GLUTEN-FREE ■ VEGETARIAN ■ BIG 8 ALLERGEN–FRIENDLY

Red peppers are one of those simple ingredients that are absolutely transformed by roasting. I have yet to find a use for them that doesn't add depth of flavor and make you reach for another bite. They're so much better than meat in this simple vegetarian sandwich.

¼ cup olive oil
8 slices ciabatta or other artisan bread, or gluten-free bread
½ cup hummus
2 roasted red peppers, thinly sliced
8 ounces halloumi cheese, sliced

1 In a large skillet, heat the oil over medium heat.

2 Slather one side of each bread slice with 1 tablespoon of hummus.

3 Divide the red peppers and halloumi among 4 of the bread slices and top with a second slice to make a sandwich.

4 Carefully transfer each of the sandwiches to the skillet and cook for about 4 minutes on each side until golden brown. Press down on the top slice of bread with a spatula. Flip carefully and repeat on the opposite side, again pressing down with the spatula.

5 Serve immediately.

SUBSTITUTION TIP: To make this gluten-free, use gluten-free bread. For a vegan sandwich, skip the halloumi.

Nutritional Information Calories: 423; Saturated Fat: 14g; Carbohydrates: 17g; Sodium: 535mg; Fiber: 3g; Protein: 17g

SMOKED TROUT
WITH ARUGULA & CREAMY DILL SAUCE ON RYE

SERVES 4 **PREP** 10 MINS **COOK** 0 MINS

■ GLUTEN-FREE

These smoky, salty little sandwiches make a substantial lunch or can be cut into triangles for an original tea sandwich. They're even better if you toast the rye bread first.

½ cup mayonnaise
1 teaspoon minced fresh dill
1 teaspoon Dijon mustard
1 teaspoon fresh lemon juice
Sea salt
Freshly ground black pepper
12 ounces smoked trout
8 slices rye bread
2 cups arugula

1 In a small bowl, whisk together the mayonnaise, dill, mustard, and lemon juice. Season with salt and pepper.

2 Toast the bread slices, if desired. Divide the trout among 4 of the bread slices. Top with the creamy dill sauce and then the arugula.

3 Top with the remaining bread slices. Serve.

SUBSTITUTION TIP: You can also use baby spinach in place of arugula. For a gluten-free sandwich, simply swap the rye bread for a gluten-free variety.

Nutritional Information Calories: 317; Saturated Fat: 3g; Carbohydrates: 14g; Sodium: 434mg; Fiber: 1g; Protein: 25g

BANH MI

■ PALEO ■ GLUTEN-FREE ■ VEGAN

In Vietnam, "banh mi" has as much meaning as "sandwich" does in the United States—it could be just about anything between two slices of bread, or for the Vietnamese, a French baguette. That said, a few ingredients are ubiquitous, flavorful, and available in many grocery stores on this side of the Pacific.

1 French baguette, cut into 4 portions
1 tablespoon sugar
Pinch sea salt
½ cup rice vinegar
2 carrots
1 (4-inch) piece Daikon radish
½ cup mayonnaise
1 tablespoon fish sauce
1 tablespoon Sriracha sauce
1 pound shredded cooked chicken
1 cup roughly chopped fresh cilantro, for serving (optional)
2 jalapeño peppers, thinly sliced, for serving (optional)

1 Preheat the oven to 375°F.

2 Arrange the bread pieces on a sheet pan and bake for 5 minutes or until warm and soft.

3 In a medium glass bowl, whisk the sugar and salt into the rice vinegar until they are completely dissolved. Julienne the carrots and daikon radish and add the julienned vegetables to the vinegar mixture to pickle them. Set aside while you prepare the other ingredients or prepare 30 minutes ahead of time and set in the refrigerator.

4 In a small bowl, whisk together the mayonnaise, fish sauce, and Sriracha.

5 Slice the bread in half horizontally and slather each cut surface with the seasoned mayonnaise. Top the bottom half of each roll with shredded chicken.

6 Drain the carrot and daikon pickles and divide them among the sandwiches on top of the chicken. Top with the fresh cilantro and jalapeño slices (if using) and top with the remaining bread slices.

COOKING TIP: Purchase a rotisserie chicken. Or better yet, make the Chicken Broth (page 32) and use the cooked chicken for the Banh Mi filling.

Nutritional Information Calories: 478; Saturated Fat: 3g; Carbohydrates: 42g; Sodium: 1231mg; Fiber: 2g; Protein: 39g

THE DIRTY DOZEN &
THE CLEAN FIFTEEN

A nonprofit and environmental watchdog organization called Environmental Working Group (EWG) looks at data supplied by the US Department of Agriculture (USDA) and the Food and Drug Administration (FDA) about pesticide residues and compiles a list each year of the best and worst pesticide loads found in commercial crops. You can refer to the Dirty Dozen list to know which fruits and vegetables you should always buy organic. The Clean Fifteen list lets you know which produce is considered safe enough when grown conventionally to allow you to skip the organics. This does not mean that the Clean Fifteen produce is pesticide-free, though, so wash these fruits and vegetables thoroughly. These lists change every year, so make sure you look up the most recent before you fill your shopping cart. You'll find the most recent lists as well as a guide to pesticides in produce at EWG.org/FoodNews.

2015 Dirty Dozen

Apples	Sweet bell peppers
Celery	
Cherry tomatoes	*In addition to the Dirty Dozen, the EWG added two foods contaminated with highly toxic organo-phosphate insecticides:*
Cucumbers	
Grapes	
Nectarines	
Peaches	
Potatoes	
Snap peas	Hot peppers
Spinach	Kale/Collard greens
Strawberries	

2015 Clean Fifteen

Asparagus	Mangoes
Avocados	Onions
Cabbage	Papayas
Cantaloupe	Pineapples
Cauliflower	Sweet corn
Eggplant	Sweet peas (frozen)
Grapefruit	Sweet potatoes
Kiwis	

APPENDIX B:
MEASUREMENT CONVERSIONS

VOLUME EQUIVALENTS (LIQUID)

US STANDARD	US STANDARD (OUNCES)	METRIC (APPROX)
2 tablespoons	1 fl. oz.	30 mL
¼ cup	2 fl. oz.	60 mL
½ cup	4 fl. oz.	120 mL
1 cup	8 fl. oz.	240 mL
1½ cups	12 fl. oz.	355 mL
2 cups or 1 pint	16 fl. oz.	475 mL
4 cups or 1 quart	32 fl. oz.	1 L
1 gallon	128 fl. oz.	4 L

OVEN TEMPERATURES

FAHRENHEIT (F)	CELSIUS (C) (APPROXIMATE)
250°F	120°C
300°F	150°C
325°F	165°C
350°F	180°C
375°F	190°C
400°F	200°C
425°F	220°C
450°F	230°C

VOLUME EQUIVALENTS (DRY)

US STANDARD	METRIC (APPROX)
$1/8$ teaspoon	0.5 mL
¼ teaspoon	1 mL
½ teaspoon	2 mL
¾ teaspoon	4 mL
1 teaspoon	5 mL
1 tablespoon	15 mL
¼ cup	59 mL
$1/3$ cup	79 mL
½ cup	118 mL
$2/3$ cup	156 mL
¾ cup	177 mL
1 cup	235 mL
2 cups or 1 pint	475 mL
3 cups	700 mL
4 cups or 1 quart	1 L

WEIGHT EQUIVALENTS

US STANDARD	METRIC (APPROX)
½ ounce	15 g
1 ounce	30 g
2 ounces	60 g
4 ounces	115 g
8 ounces	225 g
12 ounces	340 g
16 oz or 1 lb	455 g

ACKNOWLEDGMENTS

A big thanks to Clara Song Lee and Valerie Haynes Perry, whose encouragement, kindness, and editorial direction made this book what it is. To my mom, Lonnie Smith: thanks for teaching me to cook and showing me that soup is whatever you put in the pot. Thanks for sharing your recipes and love. To my mother-in-law, Debbie Ellgen: thanks for sharing your recipes and adapting your family favorites to suit our dietary preferences. To my kids, Brad and Cole: thanks for being willing to try new soups with me on this adventure! And to the chilly Pacific Ocean: thanks for giving me a really good reason to make soup.

GLOSSARY

Big 8 allergen–friendly: Recipe is free from the top eight allergens or can be adapted to be allergen-free. The Big 8 include milk, eggs, fish, shellfish, peanuts, tree nuts, wheat, and soy.

bouquet garni: A blend of two or more sprigs of herbs tied together with kitchen twine and cooked with a soup or stew. The bouquet garni is removed before serving.

brassicas: Cruciferous vegetables including cabbage, broccoli, kale, brussels sprouts, and cauliflower.

broth: A liquid created by simmering meat and/or vegetables for at least 1 hour, allowing the liquid to reduce and the flavor to intensify.

chowder: A rich soup, traditionally dairy-based and containing fish and shellfish. The definition has been expanded to include other thick rich soups, such as corn chowder.

deglaze: A technique in which meat or vegetables are browned and then wine is added to the pan and the browned bits are scraped up with a wooden spoon. Cook for 1 or 2 minutes to allow some of the alcohol to evaporate.

demi-glace: A sauce created by reducing veal or beef stock with wine and aromatics.

mirepoix: A classic trio of vegetables used to start many soups and sauces. It is composed of two parts diced onions, one part diced celery, and one part diced carrots.

purée: Soups in which all or most of the ingredients have been blended until smooth. Some purées may be topped with remaining ingredients or other garnishes.

reduction: A liquid that has been cooked uncovered until most of the liquid has evaporated to produce a highly flavorful broth or sauce.

rouille: A traditional French sauce containing red pepper and garlic that is thickened with egg yolks and bread.

roux: Equal parts butter and wheat flour whisked into a paste and cooked until bubbling. Used for thickening soups. May be cooked for 20 minutes or more to develop deep brown color and nutty flavor. Alternative fats such as canola oil or palm shortening and starchy gluten-free flours may be used.

schmaltz: Rendered chicken or goose fat often used in Central European and Jewish cuisine.

slurry: Water or broth with a small amount of flour or alternative starch whisked into it. The slurry can then be poured into a soup to thicken it. A slurry is preferable to stirring the flour directly into the soup, which may result in lumps.

soup: A combination of ingredients served in water or broth. May be cooked or uncooked.

stew: A combination of ingredients, traditionally meat, cooked in water or broth. Low, slow cooking softens tough cuts of meat.

stock: A liquid created by simmering meat or fish bones for at least 1 hour, allowing the liquid to reduce and flavor to intensify. Meat and vegetables may be added, but bones are essential. Stock adds body to soups and sauces.

sweat: Cooking vegetables, usually mirepoix, over low heat with salt to soften and release moisture without browning.

umami: A flavor imparted by glutamic acid that lends food a velvety texture on the tongue, sometimes described as a meaty flavor. It is present in monosodium glutamate, or MSG, as well as several natural sources such as celery and mushrooms.

REFERENCES

Child, Julia, Bertholle, Louisette, and Beck, Simone. *Mastering the Art of French Cooking*. New York, NY: Alfred A. Knopf, 1961.

Gayray, Khun and Gayray, Moon. *Asia Scenic Cookbook: More Than a Cookbook*. Chang Mai, Thailand: Asia Scenic Thai Cooking School Chang Mai.

McClellan, Marisa. *Food in Jars: Preserving in Small Batches Year-Round*. Philadelphia, PA: Running Press, 2011.

RECIPE INDEX

INDEX

INDEX